6,8,14,

5,7,13

VOLUNTARY NONPROFIT
ENTERPRISE MANAGEMENT

Nonprofit Management and Finance
Series Editor: VIRGINIA WHITE

A Continuation Order Plan is available for this series. A continuation order will bring delivery of each new volume immediately upon publication. Volumes are billed only upon actual shipment. For further information please contact the publisher.

VOLUNTARY NONPROFIT ENTERPRISE MANAGEMENT

David E. Mason

Supportive Services, Inc.
New Orleans, Louisiana

PLENUM PRESS • NEW YORK AND LONDON

Library of Congress Cataloging in Publication Data

Mason, David E., 1928–
  Voluntary nonprofit enterprise management.

  (Nonprofit management and finance)
  Bibliography: p.
  Includes index.
  1. Corporations, Nonprofit—Management. 2. Associations, institutions, etc.—Management.
I. Title. II. Series.
HD62.6.M37   1984   658'.048   84-17907
  ISBN 0-306-41582-8

©1984 Plenum Press, New York
A Division of Plenum Publishing Corporation
233 Spring Street, New York, N.Y. 10013

Printed in the United States of America

To Mother and Dad,
who set my course
and then let me take
hold of the tiller

PREFACE

My values, attitudes, and behaviors, like those of most Americans, have been profoundly influenced by not-for-profit enterprises. My parents were students in one when they met. I was born in one. I learned about God in one, my ABCs in another, how to make a fire and tie knots in another, how to play ball and be part of a team in another, and I met my first girlfriend in another. I prepared for my career at a not-for-profit university, met my wife at a not-for-profit church, went on to several not-for-profit graduate schools, joined numerous not-for-profit professional and special interest groups, brought two newly born sons home from not-for-profit hospitals. I read magazines published by several of them, sail and hunt with their members, and when I vote I consider a variety of their admonitions. Voluntary not-for-profit enterprises have been molding and shaping me as long as I have been alive, and they will even be represented at my funeral.

Therefore, it seems only fair that I should help to shape some of them. I have been at that task for some time now—leading seminars, consulting, writing, and serving on boards and committees. This book is an outgrowth of what I have learned through formal study, observation and analysis, and personal experience in more than half the states of the union and many foreign nations.

I wrote this book for both volunteer and paid leaders, managers, and administrators—those who make the decisions about how these diverse organizations set policy and conduct their operations. This book is for associations, schools, churches, hospitals, all sorts of charities, foundations, guilds, unions, political entities, private clubs, fraternities, ideological groups, museums, libraries, artist conglomerates, community theaters, travel groups, sports teams, professional organizations, affiliations, lobbyist groups, special interest groups, and all other not-for-profit organizations—and for individuals in the business and government sectors interested in a greater understanding of the differences in management techniques between voluntary enterprise organizations and for-profit entities.

I discovered my first book on management three years after I started managing my first not-for-profit organization. The author was writing about what I was doing every day. In a structured and comprehensive format, he outlined what I had been piecing together, bit by bit, through daily experience. The book rounded out conclusions I was just beginning to reach on my own. In one sitting I read and read, experiencing a camaraderie with the author—a recognition that "he's been there." I was discovering that I was no longer laboring alone. The book was for profit sector managers, but I was discovering that those of us in not-for-profit organizations could learn much from the literature of business management.

A decade later, I had a parallel experience. I had learned much in those intervening years. I had earned two more degrees and I was still reading books and journals on profit sector management. I was still working for a not-for-profit enterprise. As the executive director of an organization in upstate New York providing technical assistance through 17 offices in the Third World, I called a conference of leaders of other organizations working overseas. We met at the beautiful Wingspread Conference Center designed by Frank Lloyd Wright. During our first day in the relaxed and inspiring environment of the Wisconsin countryside, we got to know each other and sought to define how our organizations were similar. The second day we discussed our common needs and opportunities. I experienced the same sort of camaraderie, joy of discovery, and recognition that I had in reading my first management book. As I talked with my counterparts, I knew that they, too, "had been there." They knew the same frustrations and exhilarations I knew. They were going through what I was going through—the experience of a chief executive officer in a special kind of voluntary not-for-profit enterprise.

The first Wingspread gathering was the beginning of a series of conferences. We sought to define our commonalities. We sought to identify what made our work special—different from other professions. As a group we were a bit ahead of our time. Though the experience was great, we were not able to institute a university program in our field. We produced only one limited-circulation document (thanks to Dewitt Wallace of the *Reader's Digest*). We did not even establish a permanent organization. But from that time on, I began to think of myself not so much as the leader of a unique organization but as a voluntary enterprise manager. As such, I knew I had much in common with managers in many voluntary sector fields.

In the late 1960s I began working in New York City as a consultant for some of the largest companies in the world. Initially, it was to be a brief assignment, lasting no longer than a year. I learned much as I observed, discussed, confronted, and taught business and industrial personnel. Their status ranged from first-line supervisors through corporate vice-presidents and occasionally a president or chairman of the board. Though I highly respected the men and women with whom I worked in the profit-seeking sector, my eyes were opened to another fact. Until that time I had had an illusion that business and industry were managed better than institutions and organizations in the not-for-profit sector, in spite of the high educational level of not-for-profit managers. I had felt that business leaders were more efficient. My close association evaporated the business mystique. I found business managers more direct, realistic, and honest about motives, and more erudite than I had thought; but they were not necessarily better managers than their counterparts in the voluntary sector. They struggled with some leadership problems that would not have fazed most managers of voluntary enterprises. Many of them were relatively naive about aspects of organizational behavior. From that time, I began to make notes and gather observations on differences in effective management modes in the two sectors.

I had much help and encouragement. I learned from the organizations that shaped me and that I helped shape. I learned from my clients. I learned from my boards and my peers, and my subordinates. There are far too many to name all who provided general input. But I must mention a few who provided specific assistance: David Duhon, Bill Breedlove, Jennifer Jones, Johanna Schlater, Lucille Francis, Ellen Anderson, Steve Gurian, Darwin Fenner, Tracy Connors and fellow members of the Association of Voluntary Action Scholars, and my dear wife, who for years patiently shared our at-home hours with my work on this project.

My greatest ambition for this book is that it will provoke additional inquiry into the distinctiveness of voluntary enterprise management. Nothing would delight me more than that some of my readers would contest my conclusions, as long as there are others who have shared my kind of experience and will rise to my defense.

CONTENTS

1

VOLUNTARISM

They called it "the New World." The Western hemisphere was not merely a block of real estate, it was an opportunity for Western civilization to reshuffle its components and begin with a new deal.

Leaving most of their assets and liabilities on the European continent, a mixed bag of colonists brought to the frontier little more than their aspirations and mutual needs. But those aspirations and mutual needs were enough. For in their new environment were resources sufficient for them to win for themselves the most prosperous and democratic society the world had ever seen.

It was a new kind of society: a culture of cooperation. It was a culture comprised of people who believed in self-help, in hard work, and in voluntarily going out of their way to reach out and help those whose need required their strength. In bustling coastal cities and on the isolated frontier, they had to cooperate voluntarily in order to survive. As they moved beyond survival and into prosperity, they held onto their ethic of cooperative voluntary action. The interrelations, associations, and societies, which served them so well in survival, in prosperity made life better and richer. From the beginning, the culture of voluntary cooperation stamped the society with a special kind of heart and character.

A Culture of Cooperation

Alexis de Tocqueville, a Frenchman visiting the United States in its infancy, wrote: "These Americans are a peculiar people. In any local community a citizen becomes aware of a human need which is not being met, he thereupon discusses the situation with his neighbor. Suddenly a committee comes into existence. This committee thereupon begins to

1

operate on behalf of the need."[1] How natural it seems to us in retrospect. How striking it was to the contemporary observer!

Tocqueville also observed, "Whenever at the head of some new undertaking you see the government in France, or a man of rank in England, in the United States you will be sure to find an association." A German visitor in 1853 said, "These people associate as easily as they breathe."[2] An Englishman, James Bryce, wrote: "Associations are created, extended, and worked in the United States more quickly and effectively than in any other country. In nothing does the executive talent of the people better shine than in the promptitude wherewith the idea of an organization for common objective is taken up. . . ."[3]

In frontier committees and associations, we see that a vibrant voluntary sector has characterized us from the beginning. Most of our values, much of our nonvocational activity, our health, education, religion, culture, and welfare—and a good deal of our fun—is within this sector.

The story of voluntary enterprise weaves its way through the tapestry of history like a golden thread. When man first found that some tasks required more than one person, the result was an informal organization. Until the production of surpluses made barter possible, profit did not exist. So, by definition, the earliest organizations of man—hunting groups, family and clan, parties for foraging and defense—were nonprofit organizations. Mankind has formed itself into groups for religious purposes and to meet the demands of tribal living for thousands of years. Whenever men needed to solve a problem or seize an opportunity that required cooperation, nonprofit organizations were formed.

From the early days of Western civilization, voluntary enterprises were inexorably entwined with democracy. Greece, the cradle of democracy, also nurtured the early societies that evolved into our formally constituted modern organizations. An ancient Greek philosopher was asked, "When shall we achieve justice in Athens?" He replied, "When those who are not injured are as indignant as those who are."[4] In the early democratic milieu of Greece, membership societies of young men were experiencing the values of cooperative action. The rights of their organizations were recognized by the state, but they were not a part of the state, nor were they in business. In turn, they were a training ground for citizen involvement in the democratic process. Voluntary groups also existed in Rome, and even in the barbarian world that overran the Roman Empire.

Voluntarism landed on the American shore with the arrival of the first colonists. The 41 signers of the Mayflower Compact pledged their lives for their common cause. As settlements became communities, the cooperative society grew and flourished.

As our nation crept westward, the frontiersman awoke each morning to the sounds of the unexplored wilderness outside his western window. No matter how attached he might become to his plot of ground, there was that wistful yen to see what lay beyond the edge of the forest, to see what was beyond the nearby hill, to explore the far horizon.

On the frontier, one's past—be it rich or poor—counted for little. There was no long tradition, no established institutions upon which a weakling could depend. The challenge was always there, and the specter of the ever-present need always loomed before him. There were lands to clear, barns to raise, Indians to defend against, fields to plow, and, ultimately, hospitals, colleges, militia, and religious institutions to establish. An individual could look to no one but his comrades to meet those needs and seize those opportunities.

Women served as midwives for each other. Men took turns in burying the dead, raising new houses, and fighting fires. They set aside tracts of land to be cultivated cooperatively for community projects. Irrigation associations were voluntary enterprises to pool efforts to manage their mutual need for water for their crops. Quilting bees raised funds for schools for the children, and death-aid societies helped with funeral costs. In order to accomplish what one could not accomplish alone, the people formed voluntary groups.

It was of such a milieu that Frederick Jackson Turner said, "The effect of the frontier, has been in the promotion of democracy. . . ."[5] The frontier was not simply a place, it was a state of mind, a state of mind in which neighbor depended upon neighbor and in which a complex of voluntary associations flourished.

The Industrial Revolution modified the social structure. It paved the way for the rapid growth of the business sector and giant corporations. It created the middle class. The cooperative culture was still there. "Lady Bountiful" emerged from the parlors of the "winners" to distribute goods to the "losers." What she could not do alone could be done in cooperation with others; voluntary cooperation toward a societal good. Groups were formed, institutions were established, foundations were laid.

Prior to World War I the combined spending of the Carnegie and Rockefeller Foundations on education and social service were twice as much as that of the government! Many functions eventually absorbed by the government were initiated by the voluntary sector. For example, both the Commerce and Labor departments grew out of trade association and labor union movements.

The depression and the onset of World War II created needs on a mammoth scale. The culture of cooperation responded. It responded as it had in the abolition of slavery, in the establishment of child-labor laws, in getting the vote for women, and as it was to respond in the movement of black citizens to "overcome."

Today, even in the midst of a private sector of multinational conglomerates, and a public sector of the sprawling bureaucracies of mammoth government, the voluntary sector molds our character and gives us our "heart."

Voluntarism Today

After taking office in 1981, President Reagan called attention to voluntarism with an appeal for a rejuvenation of that culture of cooperation. He reminded us that the federal budget is not the appropriate barometer of social conscience or concern. He appealed to our distinctive character in a call to a resurgence of the tradition of citizen helping citizen and groups helping groups.

He told a story about an abnormally high tide and storm-generated surf in Newport Beach, California. "All through the day and cold winter night," he said, "volunteers worked filling and piling sandbags in an effort to save those homes. Local TV stations, aware of the drama of the situation, covered the struggle. It was about two A.M. when one newscaster grabbed a young fellow in his teens, attired only in wet trunks. He had been working all day and night—one of several hundred of his age group. No, he did not live in one of the homes they were trying to save. He was cold and tired. The newscaster wanted to know why he and his friends were doing this. The answer was poignant, and so true it should be printed on a billboard. 'Well,' he said, 'I guess it's the first time we ever felt like we were needed.'"[6] More voluntarism—and less government—is needed.

Reaction in the wake of Reagan's speech was mixed. Many applauded. They liked the idea of shifting responsibility off the shoulders of the public sector. Others were cynical, accusing the President of "setting up" the private sector to take up the slack resulting from budget cuts in social services. Others agreed with his appeal to our spirit of generous cooperation but ridiculed the idea that we could turn back the clock. "Oh, yeah? Sure the heart is there," they were saying, "but the voluntary sector is just not up to the challenge."

Indeed, the "heart" is there. A recent Gallup poll showed that Americans are volunteering more than ever. Most of us volunteer for something, some of the time. Fifty-two percent of the population is involved in some voluntary action, and 31% is "involved in organized, structured volunteerism on a regular basis."[7] The survey showed that the largest percentage of volunteers were in religious activities (19%), health (12%), and education (12%). "Upper socioeconomic groups are most likely to volunteer," the survey said. "More specifically, 63 percent of people with annual incomes of $20,000 or greater and 63 percent of the people with some college education have volunteered in the past year." Furthermore, it showed that of those volunteering, 91% also made financial contributions.

Mr. George Gallup, Jr., told me in a telephone conversation the results of a follow-up poll that his organization conducted in the Fall of 1983. This survey showed an increase in adult volunteers from 52% to 55% of the population—the growth due to an increase in the number of male volunteers.

Citizens in Arizona, Illinois, Louisiana, and across the nation are forming groups to fight crime. One community in California reported that it had cut its crime rate 20% by involving citizens in their own protection.

Businesses and labor unions are encouraging employees and members to volunteer for community service. A business group in New York found 14,000 jobs for disadvantaged youths. E. B. Industries releases employees to provide much of the emergency fire and ambulance services in Simsbury, Connecticut. Employees of Allstate Insurance have "adopted" a school in Jackson, Mississippi. I once spoke to a national convention of the Pioneers—a volunteer corps of the telephone company that performs community services. Such efforts have their public relations motives, but both management and labor leaders see it as an opportunity for the growth of individuals.

Individuals flexed their cooperative muscle when they banded together to pass California's expenditure-limiting Proposition 13. Then, when the law pulled the rug out from under many previously tax-supported services, volunteers stepped forward to help hospitals, schools, libraries, and other institutions.

A Houston ophthalmologist, Dr. Philip Weisbach, spends a week or more each year working with people with eye problems in the Third World. Dr. David Aiken, a sailing buddy of mine in New Orleans, does much the same for people with back problems, flying to Central America in his own plane.

In New York State, volunteer weather observers recently celebrated the 150th consecutive year of the efforts of their organization. My friend, Larry Ward, of Food for the Hungry, sent a ship to patrol the sea off Vietnam to save "boat people" in their foundering crafts. Mailer

Shepard in St. Louis leads a community group reversing the trend of decay in a deteriorated 700-block section of their city. Gene and Kay Boyce, of Stillwater, Minnesota, work with a group helping the families of inmates in the Minnesota State Prison. CARE fed the hungry in Poland during the reign there of martial law. New York's Economic Development Council places loaned executives in responsible slots in city government. The American Red Cross has mobilized 1.3 million volunteers for a variety of tasks.

As the voluntary sector continues to effect change, the volunteer army is itself changing. Today it spans the population from top to bottom, and from one end to the other. It includes young and old, rich and poor, liberal and conservative, black, white, red, brown, and yellow. In its ranks are corporate leaders, the President's family, movie stars, homemakers, ex-convicts, students, white- and blue-collar workers, ex-addicts, welfare mothers, and the unemployed. "For every one of those different volunteers, there is a different set of perceptions about their work, their impact, and the health of the volunteer movement," said Kenn Allen, president of VOLUNTEER, The National Center for Citizen Involvement.[8] He said:

> The story of volunteering is the story of what happens in every community every day. Those of us in the volunteer community have long recognized that ours is a broad social movement based on the interests and commitments of individual citizens. As their needs and interests change, so does the volunteer community. Constant change, an ebb and flow of programs and people, is an inevitable consequence of what volunteering is—the work of citizens in pursuit of both selfish and altruistic goals that taken as a whole build the American society.

The heart *is* there. The culture of cooperation remains imprinted on our character. But can institutionalized voluntarism meet the challenge? Can our voluntary enterprise take this spirit, this heart, and effectively supply the energy in sufficient volume to do the job? That is the question. Is a new day dawning or was the President merely a voice at sunset, calling for the impossible dream?

Just What Is Voluntarism?

In the old movie *Mr. Deeds Goes to Town*, Gary Cooper said:

> From what I can see, no matter what system of government we have, there will always be leaders and always be followers. It's like the road out in front of my house. It's on a steep hill. And every day I watch the cars climbing up. Some go lickety-split up that hill on high—some have to shift into second—

and some sputter and shake and slip back to the bottom again. Same cars— same gasoline—yet some make it and some don't. And I say the fellas who can make the hill on high should stop once in a while and help those who can't.

He was talking about the culture of cooperation. It is an ethic of self-help and hard work. But when the other fellow works hard and can't make it, or when everyone working on his own can't make it, the winners help the losers, and we all help each other. When uncoerced people come together without pay for fraternal, cultural, spiritual, social, political, or other reasons, you have voluntary action. I will use the term *voluntary not-for-profit enterprises* as a catchall term for the organizations that individuals use for cooperative voluntary action. All together, we refer to these efforts and the work of these voluntary not-for-profit enterprises as the voluntary sector.

Various classifications of voluntary not-for-profit enterprises exist— neighborhood groups, schools, museums, institutions, agencies, religious denominations, trade associations, national organizations, and the international agencies that constitute the sector. Scholars have had difficulties with definition and classification. David Horton Smith, who has broken a lot of new ground in studying voluntary action, classifies organizations into "established" organizations (nonprofit and nongovernmental, but basically nonvoluntary) that make wide use of paid staff, in contrast to "volunteer" groups, in which membership and volunteer staff predominate. He categorizes them another way as those organizations that are primarily "self-serving" in terms of the interest of the members, and "other-serving" in that their goal involves improvement of some aspect of the larger society. Organizations in the sector have also been classified as "expressive"—meeting the needs of their constituencies—and "instrumental"—meeting some societal need.[9]

Amitai Etzioni, the eminent sociologist, classifies all organizations according to their means of compliance as coercive, utilitarian, and normative. He includes most of the not-for-profit sector, both private and governmental, in the normative category. Dr. Etzioni cites nine types of organizations as follows:

> In five of these the normative pattern is highly pronounced and other patterns are relatively minor. These are religious organizations, including churches, orders, and monasteries; a sub-category of political organizations, those which have a strong ideological program; general hospitals; universities; and voluntary associations, which, as we shall see, rely mainly on social powers and commitments. Less typical, in the sense that coercion plays an important secondary role, are schools and therapeutic mental hospitals. Also less typical are professional organizations, in which remuneration plays an important part. Finally, "core" organizations of social movements

tend to have a normative compliance structure, though it is difficult to assess
its exact nature.[10]

Regardless of the classification you prefer, you must acknowledge the broad scope of the sector.

For our purposes, however, I do not think it matters. To avoid bogging down everything I say with exceptions and qualifications, I will deal with them in the aggregate, use the term *voluntary enterprise,* and let you apply what is relevant to your own organization.

The paid managers and volunteer leaders of these enterprises are a very special group. Theirs is a proud tradition. Among their ranks have been Moses, Jesus, Benjamin Franklin, George Washington, Albert Schweitzer, and Martin Luther King. There were not-for-profit organizations before there were profit-seeking ones, and before there were governments. Sociologist David S. Adams, of Ohio State University, goes so far as to say that voluntary action, such as that which takes place within voluntary enterprises, is an "authentic mode of behavior in itself."[11] It is an autonomous category of experience. As with work, play, or love, we engage in voluntary action as an end in itself, and not simply as a means to some other end.

Voluntary Enterprise Managers

Though most voluntary enterprise managers find themselves in a position they could not have defined on the day they graduated from college, they now deal with voluntary enterprise problems and opportunities. They arrived at this point by many different routes. It is likely that they have much more in common with their fellow managers than they do with those who share their original profession. By whatever road they traveled, they likely acquired their management skills in that most honored of institutions: the College of Hard Knocks.

The organizations we lead are perceived in a variety of ways. Some see them simply as ventures not efficient enough to make a profit. Others visualize them as "idealism in action," but too remote from the real world to be of interest to the pragmatic businessman. Some view them as enterprises with purposes different from business, but that otherwise can be managed in the same way, subject to the same principles and methods that work in business and industry.

How do managers in the profit-seeking sector picture their counterpart in voluntary organizations? Do they see him as a Don Quixote, jousting with windmills? As a James Jones, fleecing the innocent sheep?

Or as an Albert Schweitzer, healing those who have not even heard of medicine? Some perhaps see him as Columbus, living out his dream, to be emulated. Others barely tolerate him as an unimaginative, befuddled bureaucrat, dronishly administering his agency. Or is he viewed as a McGeorge Bundy, carrying out management functions not unlike their own?

In my childhood and youth, I at one time or another wanted to be a cowboy like Tom Mix, a buccaneer like Errol Flynn, a geophysicist like my father, or a minister like my pastor. But never during that time did I aspire to become a voluntary enterprise manager as such. So, neither did I consciously choose the role nor was I formally educated for its functions. Yet that is exactly what I became—the manager of a voluntary enterprise.

Like most of my counterparts, I began as a specialist in a profession. In graduate school I was formally educated in the traditions, ethics, expectations, and functions of that profession. After a formal induction, I began a career. Its pursuit ultimately led me to the helm of organizations made up of other professionals. Hence, I was a voluntary enterprise manager. My metamorphosis to that point was typical of many in the voluntary sector.

Association executives, college presidents, hospital administrators, bishops, heads of social service agencies, union leaders, and bureaucrats—all manage organizations that neither seek profits nor govern. Most are well educated in a professional specialty but have little formal education in management.

The Potency of Voluntary Enterprises

The culture of cooperation is essential to our free enterprise democracy. We believe that everyone should make it up that hill in front of Mr. Deeds's house on their own. But if they can't make it alone, we join together to help them help themselves. And not all of voluntarism consists of the strong helping the weak. The strong work with the strong for greater strength, and the weak work with the weak to overcome their weaknesses. In addition to social service, the voluntary sector is a vehicle for better health, for education, for recreational and cultural pursuits, and for religious and political purposes. Even the leaders of the wealthy private sector join together in trade and professional associations.

Imagine what would happen if all voluntary action were to cease. The immediate results would be bad enough. But since the sector concerns itself profoundly with values and long-term goals, the long-range result would be devastating. Our social glue is manufactured, distributed, and applied by our voluntary enterprises. We satisfy many of our hungers at their tables. It is within them that we meet our spouses, form our friendships, and entrust our children's futures. As John F. Kennedy said:

> Only by doing the work ourselves—by giving generously out of our own pockets—can we hope in the long run to maintain the authority of the people over the state—to ensure that the people remain the master; the state, the servant.
>
> Every time we try to lift a problem from our own shoulders, and shift that problem to the hands of the government, to the same extent we are sacrificing the liberties of our people.[12]

Or, as California Governor Jerry Brown said:

> The bottom line of a society is its cohesion and its sense of collective identity and common purpose. And voluntarism can make a major contribution in knitting together an increasingly separated and fragmented society. No matter how much wealth and individual accumulation there is, they can't make up for the heartache, the growing separation and consequent antagonism of a culture that can't include all the diversity that lies within it.[13]

I believe that the resources and energy for rejuvenation are within our culture of cooperation. But it must be elicited and channeled with good leadership and superior management. It cannot be done in an impersonal and mechanized manner; that is not the genius of voluntarism. We cannot depend on high government officials to do it for us. We cannot depend on the mass media to do it for us. We cannot depend on a giant of industry to do it for us. We must do it ourselves, through our local, regional, and national voluntary enterprises.

Neither the need for cooperative action nor the means for its accomplishment is diminishing. I can identify 10 indications of its potency, which can be a launching pad to a better tomorrow:

1. Man lives neither by bread alone nor by the making or selling thereof. The existence and endurance of voluntary organizations attests that it fulfills needs not otherwise met.

2. Traditionally, nonprofit organizations have been society's experimental cutting edge. Their lack of a mandate to show a profit has allowed them to pioneer new institutions and professions as their perpetually changing frontier advances into virgin territory.

3. A mammoth amount of money is involved. One recent study pegs it at 190 *billion* dollars annually. At least one-fourth of the gross national product is directly or indirectly attributable to the activities carried on by the not-for-profit sector.

4. This sector educates and trains most of the technical, professional, and managerial talent of our nation, houses much of its health care recipients, and feeds its spiritual, artistic, and nonmaterial hungers.

5. Over one-half of our population serves in this sector in some voluntary capacity. Volunteers develop leadership and organizational skills, political know-how, and self-actualization, and learn societal norms.

6. Both a successful democracy and our social system depends on the involvement of its citizens. Some observers say that if voluntary institutions cease to exist, "Democracy will have committed suicide." Our traditional image views the voluntary sector as providing this involvement by carrying out such functions as instituting information and education procedures; communicating values; bringing about orderly conflict-resolution and nonviolent confrontation; blending disparate subgroups; providing education in organizational methodology; supporting existing institutions; advocating new causes; providing mechanisms for identifying problems; feeding back opinions; instituting social reforms; building national loyalty and cohesion; guarding pluralism, altruism, self-help, and democratic action; and erecting defenses against alienation.

7. As time spent in paid work continues its apparently inevitable decline, meaningful not-for-profit involvement will claim an expanding share of the discretionary time of many of our citizens.

8. An increasingly significant portion of the work force derives its livelihood from employment outside of business and industry. One estimate indicates that it is more than one-half of all professional and technical workers in the economy, well over one-third of all service workers, and more than one-fourth of clerical workers. Not less than one-third and possibly as much as two-fifths of all employment has accounted for the activities of the not-for-profit sector.

9. They "shape and reshape the vision of a more just social order," as Ralph Kramer points out. Kramer rightly noted, "As government's role in many areas formerly dominated by nongovernmental groups grows ever larger, and the voluntary role grows correspondingly smaller, *the monitoring and influencing of government may be* emerging as one of the single most important and effective functions of the private non-profit sector."[14]

10. Voluntary organizations have deep taproots because of their noble and profound purposes. As such, they often elicit great commitment and loyalty. The challenges faced by the voluntary sector today are as great as or greater than those at any time in history. Can we meet the challenges?

   I believe the answer lies in applying management skills to the task. Superior management can do for the voluntary sector in the years ahead what it has done for the private sector in the years past. It can take the resources of our culture of cooperation, while the heart for it is still beating, and apply those resources to the task with efficiency and effectiveness. It can—if we *adapt* the best of what the world has learned about management in business and industry and use it to elicit and apply the energy of voluntarism toward a rejuvenated society.

   This book is for those who would lead the voluntary sector into a new day, whether they be paid voluntary enterprise managers or volunteers at the policy or administrative levels. I am bullish on voluntarism. But I think the sector must dramatically improve its management skills. In this book I will point the way. It is not large enough to be a storeroom for all the know-how required. But I think it can help to open the door.

2

A DISTINCTIVE MANAGEMENT
APPROACH

"Perhaps the greatest challenge we face today, in the Western world," according to the eminent management consultant Peter Drucker, "is to improve the managerial performance of the non-profit institutions."[15] The enterprises in the voluntary sector are, in my opinion, the best vehicles available to carry us forward together toward better societies made up of more fulfilled individuals. But while the potential of the vehicle is there, it may not yet function well enough to make the trip required of it.

Voluntary not-for-profit organizations are not businesses. They have different purposes, different natures, different value systems, and they succeed or fail in different ways.

After World War II, the business sector experienced a "management boom," resulting in a complete overhaul of business management indicators, goals, concerns, and systems. A similar insurgence of management methods is essential if the voluntary enterprises are going to transform themselves from what they are to what they can become.

Many business executives, educated in the management sciences and effective in their own positions, superficially survey the operations of a not-for-profit enterprise and—seeing practices they would not tolerate in their own businesses—they react: "If I ran my business like this outfit is run, we'd be bankrupt in a week!" They are probably right. Running a business like a voluntary enterprise would be as disastrous as running a voluntary enterprise like a business.

A survey conducted by the American Institute of Management was particularly critical of the management of religious organizations. It reported that "viewed against the background of modern business corporations, the management practices of religious organizations are appallingly archaic."[16] Yet I recently saw the first telephone directory published in New Orleans. All of the churches in the directory are extant, while fewer than a dozen of the businesses are still operating! During 1982 not one of the 1,000 churches in Greater New Orleans went out of business because of the recession. How many business failures were there? Still, many business leaders look upon their volunteer sector counterparts as amateurs. Such business managers are in a venerable tradition. Back in days of Louis XIV, Colbert blamed the problems of a service institution on its lack of "business-like" management. Colbert applied business systems and achieved phenomenal early success. Unfortunately, he forgot that voluntary enterprises—in this case Louis's voluntary penchant for wars—cannot be measured by the same yardstick. He was doomed ultimately to fail. Both the modern businessman and Colbert would have been ahead of the game had they prescribed "better management" rather than "business-like" management. Management, yes. But "like business," no.

Voluntary enterprises require distinctive management systems. Many management practices, perfectly effective in business, *must be adapted* before they will work in voluntary enterprises. Management is management, and shoes are shoes, but shoes work better when sized to the appropriate feet. A checker player, upon first seeing a chess set on his familiar checkerboard, might mistakenly assume that, but for the form of the pieces, the two games are alike. Indeed, the boards are identical. Each game is played with the same number of "men," placed initially on the same squares on the board, and they are moved from square to square by people who may be seated in the same kind of chairs. But the objectives are different, the powers of the pieces are different, and to win, you must make different moves.

What Is Management?

I learned early in life that not everyone with the title "manager" performs management functions, and that many managers do not have that particular word in their titles. I was little more than a child when I first encountered the term. A certain gangling, Adam's-apple type of boy was pointed out as the manager of the football team. I was amazed that such an obvious nonjock would be associated with that rough-and-tumble sport. Then a friend told me that all there was to the team manager's job was to help the coach look after helmets, shoulder pads, and towels. No more than a month later I joined the staff of the school paper. On my first day, the faculty advisor introduced the newcomers to the staff. There was the editor, the sports reporter, the gossip colum-nist—how impressed I was to be in the same room with these junior-high-school celebrities. Everyone in the school knew their names and read their writings. As a new general flunky, I knew there was a chance that perhaps the next year I might fill one of their seats. At last, the faculty advisor came to the final introduction—the business manager. I had never noticed her name in the paper, had never seen anything she wrote, and never found out what she did. But I was beginning to get the idea about managers! They were not really very important to the real action.

You can imagine how confused I was later when my parents pre-pared me for a visit from my father's manager. "Big deal . . . a manag-er," I thought. But when I had to wash the car and help mow the yard, and saw all of the dusting, cleaning, cooking, and dressing up about me, my brain whirled. It turned out he was a vice-president of Standard Oil who had come all the way from New York. Somehow he held the fate of our family in his hands.

Eventually, I sorted it out in my mind. Real managers sit at steering wheels to make things happen. The coach was the real manager of the football team. The faculty advisor was the real manager of the school paper. My father's manager was his boss, and my father was the manag-er of that part of the company in which he worked.

Management is hard to define in a comprehensive and truly satisfy-ing way. There are many definitions because the mass of knowledge about it is still growing and shifting about. A definition that is exactly right has not coalesced from that mass, but it is easily described. It is an integrating set of functional responsibilities that operate continuously over time, getting things done through people in an organizational sys-tem. It is that component of an enterprise charged with performing critical functions for success. It charts the course and is responsible for bringing the big ship safely into port. Management includes leadership in motivating and directing others. It is, therefore, terribly important and essential to the success of any venture.

Management is answering the questions: What do we want? What shall we do? How shall we do it? It is the activity of applying the resources to the accomplishment of the tasks of the organization. Suc-cessful management is doing so in such a way that the benefits are optimal, the costs minimal.

Approaching management from several directions, we see that it is that component of an organization that studies, analyzes, and makes decisions regarding what the business of the organization is and should become. It is responsible for the effectiveness and efficiency of the enterprise, and it has the authority to apply resources to meet organizational goals. Its expertise requires such processes as planning, organizing, staffing, directing, motivating, and controlling. Management utilizes such methods as marketing and operational research, productivity evaluation, cost–benefit analysis, systems analysis, program evaluation and review, and management by objectives. (Management in the voluntary sector includes a double portion of what we call *leadership*. Voluntary enterprises have to accomplish what their business counterparts do without always paying their workers.)

The terms *management* and *administration* are often used interchangeably. Business tends to use *management* and *manager* while government and the voluntary sector tend to use *administration* and *administrator*. But more and more, the terms are evolving to refer to two different levels of making things happen. *Management* implies more self-determination, a greater control of resources, and more creativity. Administration connotes the carrying out of executive details, of operating and maintaining that which is "given." Management has more to do with the selection of goals; administration, the attainment of those goals. I prefer the term *management* as the broader, more conceptual term, and will so use it.

Management is to the organization what the mind is to the nervous system. The management team profoundly affects the fate of the enterprise. Two businesses, similar but for management, can move in dramatically different directions. In a few years, one may crash like Braniff while another, like Southwest Airlines, sees its stock soar. K-Mart can grow to become the second largest retailer while Woolco closes its doors.

Good management made the difference between a McDonald's that was a single hamburger joint and one whose golden arches spanned the world; between Sony and Datsun remaining small Japanese firms or threatening General Electric and General Motors; between you lining your dresser drawers with Xerox stock, or retiring on it. Bad management is the reason your mother could put down her *Look* magazine, get into her Studebaker, drive to W. T. Grant's department store, and buy a Muntz television set, and you can't. Good management has brought reliable phone service, comfortable air travel, year-round fresh food on the shelf, and monthly credit-card bills that arrive on time. Bad management provides appliance repairs that cost a fortune, hours of sitting in waiting rooms, ensnarled city traffic, and bureaucratic foul-ups. Good management on the part of Japanese automobile manufacturers allowed their small cars to invade and occupy one-third of the United States market. The quality of management is the watershed that separates crowning success from drowning failure.

Management Functions

Managers operate at many levels. The supervision of the smallest unit in an organization must be managed well if that unit is to do its job. Every functional department and every geographical branch has a manager. The dollar value of decisions, the number of employees, and the size of the physical plant can vary, but management principles apply on each level, and on each a manager is responsible for results.

The characteristic differences in management functions between business and voluntary enterprises are sufficiently profound to require distinctive management.

In spite of the proliferation of voluntary nonprofit enterprises, this sector is perceived by many to be ill-managed. Indeed, they often are if management activities of not-for-profit organizations are evaluated against the yardstick of business.

A columnist in the *Wall Street Journal* reflected a typical business attitude toward the management of voluntary enterprises when she wrote: "The whole subject of . . . volunteer efforts is terminally boring. Volunteer activity so often absorbs itself in the small particulars of situations; . . . we have become impatient with this sort of smallness."[17]

I have been "in business" for much of my working life, running a consultant organization dealing with some of the largest corporations in America, as well as small and medium-size businesses. I have also been concerned with making a profit in real estate, ranching, and mineral properties. And I know that there is an uneven image of voluntary not-for-profit enterprises and their managers. While I do not agree that the smoky image is entirely accurate, where there is smoke, there is need for a fire extinguisher.

I have seen an awareness growing in the ranks of voluntary enterprise leaders over the last two decades. College presidents are learning that their jobs have more in common with the job of a museum director than with that of one of their professors. Bishops see their commonality with heads of service agencies. Hospital administrators find that they can learn from the experience of a Chamber of Commerce executive. Association executives are aware that, although their constituencies are quite different from one another, their own operations are quite similar. More than ever before, those whose job it is to lead a variety of organizations are beginning to see themselves as managers, managers of voluntary not-for-profit enterprises, and to realize that their problems and the management required to solve them represents a distinctive discipline.

Many business principles have been used successfully in the voluntary sector. Others have distorted, maimed, or created dissension in perfectly good institutions. The difficulties were caused because of a lack of clear understanding of the differences in the two sectors. Also, management as a distinct discipline has only recently begun to emerge in not-for-profit organizations. The management sciences have ignored voluntary enterprise management as a specialized field. But in the last decade, there has been an increasing pressure from funding agencies, regulatory bodies, foundations, and corporate and individual contribution sources for objective evidence of organizational effectiveness. We are moving out of an era when money was given for promises, and into an era when effective management and objective evaluation is a precondition to funding. So voluntary enterprise managers are motivated to improve their skills.

They have taken advantage of the literature, have attended management seminars, and have adapted some of the more popular management fads to which they have been exposed. Generally, they have benefited. They have found that many of the principles and methods suggested make their work more effective. But often they find that, as with hand-me-down clothes, the fit is not quite right; it is like the square peg in the round hole.

Voluntary enterprises are *not* businesses. They have their own distinctive characteristics, which require a distinctive management program. Before the wealth of management information can be adapted successfully, you must understand what the distinctive characteristics of voluntary enterprises are.

Why the Business Model?

If the management of voluntary enterprises is different from business management, then why refer to the business management model at all?

Business management research has leapfrogged voluntary enterprise expertise by a tremendous bound in this century. Not only can much of business management knowledge be applied directly to the management of voluntary enterprises, but other aspects of the business model can also be adapted. Though many businesses continue to work by seat-of-the-pants instinct, and many operate by management folklore that cannot stand up under objective evaluation, there is a wealth of solid knowledge available. Proven principles exist in such quantity, in fact, that many voluntary enterprise managers could significantly increase their own effectiveness by systematic application of gleanings from this field of knowledge.

Here are several reasons why the profit-seeking model is the best starting point:

1. As the management authority Peter Drucker points out, "Business management is the success story of this century. It has provided economic goods and services to an extent that would have been unimaginable in the generation of 1900. And it has performed despite world wars, depressions, and dictatorships."[18]

2. In business and industry, improvements in efficiency and effectiveness pay off in dollars. Since investment in improved methodology pays, vast amounts have been spent in identifying better methods.

3. The common denominator in both types of organization (business and not-for-profit enterprises) is people. Therefore, concepts that have been identified in business in many cases can be applied to volunteers and voluntary associations.

4. Management has reached its apogee in industry with its measurable outputs. Rationalization withers away in the light of the unambiguous feedback of the marketplace.

5. Management experts operating within business and industry have access to large numbers of cases. They base their studies on extremely costly operations that rarely can be duplicated in studies elsewhere.

6. Incentives for universities, consultants, and other "outsiders" to research business management are so great that the outputs of their research have been almost exclusively for the benefit of business.

7. As J. Malcolm Walker of San Jose State University has pointed out, business provides monetary incentives, the dependence of employees on earnings, and the formal structures of accountability, which greatly facilitate the control of human behavior and hence produce greater reliability in research findings.[19] The profit motive that permeates virtually all aspects of a business organization provides direct realistic feedback for the objective evaluation of results.

These are some of the reasons why the profit-seeking model is an obvious starting point and why I recommend that a voluntary enterprise manager use the business model as a basis from which to adapt.

On the other hand, why should a manager in the business sector be interested? Cognizant of more management principles than he is able to utilize in his own business, why should he concern himself with voluntary enterprise management?

For one reason, he could want to apply his own management skills more effectively as a leader in a voluntary organization he serves, be it a university, trade association, church, club, or advocacy group. As a contributor, as a civic leader, or as part of his corporate function, he might need to evaluate nonprofit organization management accurately to make proper decisions concerning such organizations. He might be interested because of the importance of this sector to our way of life, as shown in the Gallup poll cited in Chapter 1.

Voluntary enterprises have contributed much to the American culture. Our nation began with a call to volunteer minutemen to defend against paid professionals. These professional mercenaries were set upon us because a volunteer group dumped tea belonging to a business into Boston Harbor. Voluntarism has persisted and is now entrenched.

Beginning in late 1978, graduate business schools such as Harvard, Stanford, and Columbia reported an acceleration of graduates interested in not-for-profit work. The popularity of MPA (Master of Public Administration) programs is evidenced by an increasing student population.

While Harvard and Columbia MBA's previously evinced little interest, more than 20% of their beginning classes now seek employment in not-for-profit organizations.[20] Says Ray Horton of Columbia University, "Last year we had a dozen people show up for an orientation meeting for non-profits. Now we have about 80 percent."[21]

Finally, the business manager should be concerned because nonprofit organizations are often characterized by uneven performance. They need help in adapting management knowledge to their kind of enterprise. Though many are successful by any measure, we can concede that in our modern era of sorting fact from folklore, business management science has often surpassed the leadership of service organizations. Richard Cornuelle, when with the National Association of Manufacturers, wrote, "Today the independent sector stands about where the commercial sector stood in the centuries before we knew why it worked."[22] I agree with his prophecy that such organizations constitute the real growth-sector of a modern society.

An organization is a body of interacting persons who anticipate that the benefits of association will be greater than its cost.

Distinctive Characteristics

The voluntary not-for-profit sector, the governmental or public sector, and the private or business sector are all vital to our society. But their organizations are distinctly different in their purpose, their nature, and the way they are operated. Each sector depends upon the others. Each can learn from the others.

The principles here are for those who are responsible for leading voluntary not-for-profit enterprises, whether they be professional managers on the organization's staff or persons from the other sectors who serve in volunteer leadership capacities. The contents will be built around those characteristic differences between voluntary enterprises and profit-seeking enterprises, differences that mandate a distinctive management for each. Only by fully understanding these differences can we adapt the best that is available in the management sciences to the voluntary sector.

Drawing upon 25 years of experience as a manager and as a consultant in both the profit-seeking and the not-for-profit sectors, and upon extensive study and feedback during seminars and workshops, I have identified 14 major characteristic differences between voluntary not-for-profit enterprises and profit-seeking businesses.

These may not be all of the differences between not-for-profit enterprises and their profit-seeking counterparts. Some are even derivative of others. They are not of equal rank. But they are all differences, and they do require management incongruent with traditional business principles. In some cases, the difference is only a matter of degree, but then so is the difference between Shirley Temple and Bo Derek.

Eleven of my 14 characteristics served as a basis of a study by David Duhon, then of Louisiana State University.[23] His study verified that the characteristics were acceptable to a randomly selected sample of management scholars, business managers, and not-for-profit managers.

The characteristics, which we will consider in subsequent chapters, are as follows:

1. The market value of the services of voluntary enterprises cannot be measured as precisely as in business.
2. Their purposes are other than profit-seeking.
3. Their principal tool is volunteerism produced by persuasion.
4. The production of resources and the provision of services are two distinct systems, whereas in business the systems are integrated.
5. Voluntary enterprises have a special kind of constituency.
6. Money is a means in the voluntary sector, while in business it is an end.
7. Not-for-profit groups enjoy a special legal status.
8. Voluntary enterprises do not have a profit-and-loss criterion with which to monitor operational effectiveness.

9. Management requires more diplomacy. In business, management has more autonomy.
10. Voluntary enterprises tend to accumulate multiple purposes.
11. Voluntary enterprises have a distinctive social charater.
12. The resources available to not-for-profit groups are not as limited as business resources.
13. The groups can persist even though their consumption of resources consistently exceeds their tangible output.
14. Voluntary enterprises are characteristically more complex than their business counterparts.

3

MANAGEMENT MEASURABILITY AND THE IMMEASURABLE

There is measure in all things.

Horace, *Satires*[24]

Long before the development of commerce, our remote ancestors had already found that they could accomplish more by cooperating in small groups than by laboring alone. Hunting in bands enabled them to kill the larger animals with relative safety. They could defend themselves better when several families lived together. So the family, clan, hunting group, and primitive arrangements for specialization and the exchange of goods—subsistence barter—existed as nonprofit entities prior to the establishment of either profit-making organizations or government. Not until a surplus developed was it possible to have profit. Government was necessary in order to enforce matters that were for the common good but that required some form of coercion.

With the advent of profit-seeking, activities that were undertaken previously on a cooperative, not-for-profit basis began to change by moving into the realm of business. This included the distribution of virtually all tangible items. Goods—unlike services—are easy to weigh and measure, and market values can be quickly established. If a measurable value of a service could be established in the marketplace, it too could be provided by a profit-seeking enterprise. But a service, unlike tangible goods, cannot always be taken home as the exclusive property of the purchaser. Some services provide value to society as a whole. There remained needs that, while important to the society, were difficult to assign a value. Some, such as child care and education, were provided by the family. Others, such as tradition (mores and customs), were handled by the society as a whole, through acceptance or ostracism, punishment or reward. Government provided peace-keeping and defense from enemies. Religious institutions attended to spiritual affairs, and a wide range of services later spun off into a variety of educational, cultural, governmental, health, and welfare organizations. The not-for-profit organizations, in the aggregate, are often said to compose the *third sector* (after business and government), when in reality they were the first sector.

When a service evolved to the point where its market value became measurable, an entrepreneur would often find a way of making a profit. At this point the service would often move from the not-for-profit into the profit-seeking sphere. The only way an individual could risk getting into business was to predict a reasonably certain market value. Today, voluntary not-for-profit enterprises continue to have a monopoly on the unpredictable, ambiguous, vaguely defined, intangible, and difficult-to-measure service.

I believe this is why we have voluntary enterprises. It is the reason undergirding this sector. In an age of big government and big business, it is the reason that not-for-profit organizations persist.

We have voluntary enterprises because resources have been available to support organizations providing services for which *the market value is not measurable.* It is that simple. That is why we have organizations as diverse as Harvard University, the Metropolitan Museum of Art, the Kidney Foundation, Goodwill Industries, and the Mother's Day Out program at the Presbyterian Church around the corner.

Market-value measurability is the watershed that separates the not-for-profit sector from the profit-seeking sector. *The market value of the services of voluntary enterprises cannot be measured as precisely as can the outputs of business enterprises.* This characteristic is a primary distinction between the two classes of organizations. It is this characteristic that keeps the less measurable values in the not-for-profit province. This same characteristic makes it difficult to evaluate the performance of the not-for-profit organizations.

Some argue that "purpose" is the prime cause underlying the voluntary sector. I might agree, except for the way the voluntary sector pioneers, develops, then loses whole classes of services to business once a market value is established. For example, consider what happened in the environmental pollution area. When the antipollution laws were passed in the 1960s and early 1970s, the work was done by public and private not-for-profit enterprises. Today, hundreds of businesses are profiting in this field. Profit-seeking entrepreneurs and professionals are readily available whenever a market value becomes clearly defined. Without thinking, many feel that the voluntary sector has a corner on things like health, education, and culture. But those same services are, to some degree, provided at a profit within the business sector. The components that remain in the voluntary sector are those for which an unpredictable market exists.

Once voluntary enterprises became identified as that sector of the society with a certain portfolio, needs of a certain type tended to be referred to organizations and institutions in the sector. Their style and proficiency at meeting a particular type of need attracted to the not-for-profit format a wide range of associations, societies, and agencies. As long as someone was willing to support their work, they continued on the experimental cutting edge, working in areas such as health, education, welfare, culture, and religion.

There are other needs that require the rule of law, or for which not enough voluntarily contributed support is available. In such cases, they fall to the governmental sector. Though there is much overlap, as not-for-profit departments exist within business organizations and businesses can be owned by voluntary enterprises, the lack of measurable market value continues as the fountainhead of the not-for-profit sector.

The "scientific method" is credited with changing history and with creating much of the difference in the quality of life between advanced and underdeveloped cultures. It is also the foundation of modern management. In gradually sorting fact from fantasy, it leads, step by step, toward improved methods. A reminder of what it is and how this reasoning process works will emphasize the value of measurable outputs.

The steps in the process of the scientific method are as follows:

1. The event is defined. (In voluntary management, for example, we might specify the need to improve the carpentry skills of a group of prisoners.)
2. We make observations. (We define the activities in our carpentry training program and similar programs.)
3. We develop a hypothesis that attempts to explain the relationship among the variables observed. (Our hypothesis might be that skills will improve if the prisoners work on projects that they can later use instead of those that must be left in the shop.)
4. An experiment tests the hypothesis. (We have half the prisoners work on projects that they can keep or send to their families, and the other half works on projects that will remain in the shop.)
5. The results are measured. (We test all of the prisoners for skill levels before and after the experiment, and compare their relative progress.)
6. The results prove the hypothesis correct or incorrect. If it is

correct, the hypothesis is accepted as a valid explanation for the events studied. If not, a new hypothesis must be formulated and tested.

Note how essential measurement is, if the scientific method is to be used. It is the key to decisionmaking.

Aspects of Measurability

Examine now some of the aspects of the lack of measurability on the market value of voluntary enterprise outputs. We will then consider some of the management implications.

If an organization is responsible for services for which the value is not as measurable as in profit-seeking business, it has no mandate to make a profit. This gives it a freedom and a flexibility that business lacks. A voluntary enterprise can deal in a variety of unmeasurable values and benefits. After all, there is more to life and society than what can be measured. Consider, for example, the things that have meant most to you. While unmeasurable values do not become the exclusive property of the nonprofit groups, they have a degree of license to immerse themselves in the benefits of such values.

We have not yet found absolute measures for a child's happiness, a successful marriage, a youth's education, an adult's health, friendship, pleasure, or job satisfaction, an older person's feeling of appreciation, comfort, or contentment. How do we measure the morale of a society, the patriotism of a population, the loyalty or motivation of a work force? We do not attempt to assign numbers to degree of hope, faith, or love. We have no market-value measurement for the feeling of belonging and comradeship, or the satisfaction of making a significant, meaningful, and worthwhile contribution to a cause. The voluntary enterprise has outputs in subjective utility, emotional payoffs, and cultural enrichment. Just because these intangible values are not measurable does not mean they lack worth.

Humanity has been greatly enriched by the outputs of the voluntary sector—outputs that are obviously valuable in the long-term retrospect, though unmeasurable in the short-term. The sector provides a seedbed for new ideas and approaches to take root, mature, and yield fruit that years later proves their worth. Only with the passage of time can the good be sorted from the worthless, and the value of the ideas truly appreciated. The time-span is too long for a prudent investor seeking a return on his capital. For example, venture capitalists, the high-risk-takers who finance businesses, usually seek to recover their investment within three years. So society, without a guarantee of return, continues to invest for the long-term good. Voluntary enterprises will persist as long as resources are made available to support efforts for which the short-term market value is unmeasurable. After all, quantifiable measurements of short-term objectives can be short-sighted. We don't evaluate Columbus's contribution to the world on whether or not he reached the Indies!

Malcolm Walker, of San Jose State University, reminded me of some of the advantages of working in organizations with a soft measurability of outputs.[25] Individuals who want to do good, to make significant changes, to provide services when there are none, can do so in a voluntary enterprise. If a profit had to be made, there would not be as great an opportunity to pioneer. Voluntary enterprise managers can be considerably more flexible, creative, and imaginative than their profit-seeking counterparts. Such organizations provide a wider range of motivations for doing things, and therefore a broader scope in opportunities for satisfaction and accomplishment.

However, the weakness in measurability can be a management nightmare. When results are harder to measure, they are also harder to attain. How do you establish standards and measure performance against them? If there is no absolute measure in the market place, neither are measures always available for choosing among alternatives, for arriving at an equitable price structure, for determining true benefits, for comparing with the past, for forecasting the future, for comparing across organizational lines, for collaborating with other sectors, and for accounting to funding sources.

Involved as they are with services subject primarily to subjective evaluation, voluntary enterprises can become an environment enjoying a lack of objective reality. Employees can revel in the processes of their professions—in the joys of study, the complexities of human relations, and the satisfactions of activity—without being aware of their lack of stewardship of the resources entrusted to their care. Activity can be stressed over accomplishment, inputs over outputs, and a pervasive indifference can exist to the relationship of costs to benefits. The sincerity, goodwill, and concern of the service providers can override the true needs of the clients in a climate of carelessness.

Quantitative Measurement Problems

Voluntary organizations are characteristically "living systems," with much interaction with the environment of the society. This interfacing makes them highly subject to change as they influence and are influenced. With this type of organization it is hard to establish absolute causal relationships. Subjective thinking, value judgments, and intuition are often more appropriate bases for action than quantitative data. At best, many of the quantitative measures deal with only a few of the situational facts. To respond to them alone is to fail to grasp the entire picture. Group opinion is highly significant, process has more weight than in business, and implications for the constituents and contributors have to be considered in addition to the tastes and needs of the clients. In such an organization, measurements can serve to reduce the variables and assist in decision making, but they are not the only dimension.

The outputs of the voluntary sector also often have a societal value. If management is to accurately measure the value of these outputs, it must measure the social benefits in addition to the benefits to individual recipients. Even the output in relation to an individual or a family are multiple and difficult to measure in terms of a single aspect.

The measurability problem is often the result of many variables with which the manager must deal. Without absolute output measures, he could see his organization through rose-colored glasses. Objective reality can be hidden in the morass of subjective data. He can be lulled into a state of complacency or even optimism when it is not warranted. He can make serious errors in judgment, and a detrimental amount of time can elapse before errors are noted. The lack of a true market test can sap an organization of its self-discipline. A trickle of anecdotal information can give the constituency a distorted view of reality. For example, well-intentioned organizations with ineffectual controls may spend inordinate proportions of their resources in fund-raising. Their service purpose may even be sidetracked due to their funding efforts. On the profit-seeking side, the measurable marketplace forces a business to face reality, abandon uneconomic products, and meet new needs, or be forced into bankruptcy.

Qualitative Measurement Problems

The qualitative nature of many of the outputs of service organizations is part of the problem. Quality is rarely subject to addition, multiplication, or division. Red and yellow are not necessarily twice the value of yellow alone. A sound that is 30% louder is not necessarily 30% better. Spending twice as much time on an operation does not mean that the result is twice as good, nor does spending half as much time on it make it more efficient. If a public health center increases its number of patients by 25% does this mean it is one-fourth more effective? Would a reduction of the load indicate that it is doing a better job?

We have not yet developed an acceptable quantitative measure of health, but we can measure the number of patients treated. We cannot measure the effectiveness of education, though we can measure the amount of preparation by the faculty, the student–teacher ratio, and the number of hours spent with students. In other words, we can measure inputs easier than we can measure outputs. In a culture that emphasizes numbers there is a tendency to measure activity and process rather than results. This can lead management down a long and wasteful road. Managers can often be satisfied with a "good reason" because of the difficulty in finding the *right* reason.

As results are difficult to measure, they can be more difficult to attain. Moon Landrieu, when he was secretary of HUD in the Carter administration, spoke to me about his voluntary sector experience: "The measurement of our success is not as clear as it is with private companies."[26] Without measurement, how can the performance of an employee be accurately assessed? Is he to be measured by how well he is liked, by how hard he seems to work, by how popular he is with the board, or by how well he writes up his accomplishments?

There is a tendency in such an environment for staff members to be given responsibility for certain functions rather than for obtaining certain results. Managers rarely have sufficient objective data by which to choose among alternatives. Not only is the relationship between costs and benefits difficult to determine, it is often difficult to identify accurately the amount of benefits.

What Are the Solutions?

Many implications in the lack of measurability are laid at the doorstep of the voluntary enterprise manager. This is further complicated because he often has a problem in getting outside assistance. Management literature, management scholars and consultants, and educational opportunities are usually oriented to management by measurable objectives.

The business executives who serve as volunteers on their boards or on various committees are also accustomed to managing by quantifiable objectives. They are often completely disoriented in an environment with so many unmeasurable items, and they make recommendations that are not always helpful to the organization's purpose. This can create additional problems. Measurement for measurement's sake is time-wasting at least, and can be disastrous. Whether or not you measure the right thing makes all the difference. Measuring Einstein's height, Roosevelt's running speed, or Madam Curie's sex appeal would have distorted the evaluation of them all.

Or take an example for the automobile industry. In the early 1970s, the president of American Motors compared the size of his company with that of other major corporations and noted how much larger American Motors was than companies in other fields. He concluded that his company, therefore, was in good shape. But American Motors was not in the food business, like General Mills, or the textile or paper business. It was in the automobile business, like General Motors and Ford, and had an insignificant share of the market. American Motors was not in good shape, and within a decade it had to be bailed out by Renault.

This characteristic affects the overall thrust of an organization, especially its decision-making procedures and its planning and control functions. In a culture that increasingly places a premium on measures, the manager is under pressure to produce on items that are quantifiable to the neglect of those that are not. This may cause a manager to measure what is easily measurable rather than what is significant. He may measure inputs instead of outputs, processes rather than results, or may modify otherwise significant activities to satisfy a need for "better numbers."

For instance, an agency may resort to "creaming" when under pressure to produce the right numbers. This is the practice of working on the easiest or most lucrative cases in order to show immediate measurable results instead of addressing the cases that should be of central concern. An agency charged with training unskilled, untrained, and unemployed ghetto youth and placing them in jobs where they can function and become taxpayers instead of tax-consumers began to fall behind in its quota. It solved the problem by "creaming" when it began recruiting marginal individuals who might well have succeeded on their own. The agency turned its back on the hard cases in order to show clearly measurable results.

An organization has inputs (that which enters its system), transformations (interventions that take place within the system), and outputs (the result of the transformation). Measurement of the output is the measure of the results of its work. But often you will find an inappropriate concentration on input, which can be measured, to the neglect of output, which cannot. Recognition of this potential pitfall should be formalized in writing. This will minimize the tendency to ignore it in the planning and decision-making processes. It will be a hedge against a tendency for the organization to drift away from its purposes.

The starting point is to have a clear definition of the organization's purposes. Then the manager can begin to deal with the problems precipitated by the relative lack of measurability. With written mission statements and goals, the leadership can determine how well the enterprise is functioning with respect to its purposes. Goals and objectives must include not only those outputs on the more tangible and measurable end of the scale but also those on the other end—attitudes and concepts that are unmeasurable. An honest recognition of the expressive needs of the constituency should also be included.

In many enterprises, the original reason for its establishment was to provide meaningful participation for a group of persons. If this continues as an organization purpose, it should be included in the statement of goals and objectives. Clarification of purpose is vital if the leadership is to respond effectively to the difficulty in managing an enterprise that cannot absolutely measure the market value of its outputs. There must be a relatively high degree of certainty as to what the organization is seeking to accomplish. These goals should be written, whether or not they have external manifestation.

With written purposes and goals in hand, each can be studied and decisions can be made as to how management can determine progress in relation to them. The leadership can then determine which organizational outputs are truly unmeasurable and which ones are indeed measurable. By establishing measures for some, the degree of uncertainty is reduced, and those items that can only be evaluated subjectively can be given their proper weight. Management will probably discover that more of the organization's outputs are measurable than they previously thought. They should establish standardized procedures to quantify measurable outputs, so the enterprise can take advantage of all that measurable objectives offer.

Once the item to be measured has been unambiguously defined, procedures and a standard unit of measure should be designated. Everyone will then be measuring the same thing and will get comparable answers. With the service-providing system of a voluntary enterprise, this may be called a "service unit." It will be a finite basic subdivision of one of the organization's objectives. For instance, it might be a grade level of educational attainment, one point on an attitudinal scale, a child placed for adoption, or a patient who has been symptom-free for a year. In selecting the units to be used, the definition and the assignment of weight or value is critical.

Van Gigch[27] suggests six questions to be considered in defining such units of measure:

1. Is the definition unambiguous enough that two people will interpret it in the same way without requiring further explanation?

2. Does the definition include or imply a procedure by which it can be measured?
3. Does the procedure describe the standard conditions under which measurement must be obtained? Are the procedures easy or difficult to replicate?
4. Are the methods of measurement such that the same numerical value will be obtained by all those attempting the measurement?
5. Does the measurement provide decision-makers with a clear picture of the events in such a way that they are helped in their policy choices?
6. Does the measurement provide an idea or a direction of causality among the factors measured?

Even many previously unmeasurable items might be quantified by recently developed techniques. There is a beginning to the measurement of the "soft" systems that we often find in voluntary enterprises. True, they are measured along weaker scales than are outputs of "hard" systems. But special methods can be devised to cope with this limitation in many cases.

Also, there are *manifestations* of intangible goals that are measurable even though the goals themselves are not. For instance, you cannot measure a goal such as "to provide for a more meaningful life for the handicapped." But you can measure the number of paraplegics who are placed in jobs. You may not be able to measure "art appreciation for the disadvantaged," but you can measure the number of neighborhood children who graduated from a Saturday morning class. After all, a thermometer does not directly measure the temperature of the air. Rather, it measures the manifestation of that temperature as it affects the height of a column of mercury.

It is important to recognize that the measurability problem should not simply be written off because of its difficulty. While it is not always possible to quantify goals, and much hard thinking is required to develop alternative management tools, a commitment must be made to the struggle. Only then can real, rather than imagined, progress ensue. So, even though all may not be measurable, those outputs that can be, should be. Obviously, the fewer items that remain ambiguous and unmeasurable, the more productive decision making will be.

The measurement of inputs in the form of resources made available to an organization is a poor measure of its provision of services. The measurement of intermediate outputs is a step in the right direction. By intermediate outputs I mean the results of the productivity of the organization's staff and volunteers. While this is usually at least one step removed from the value of the service to the clientele, it is often more readily measurable. Some examples are the number of homes participating in an anticrime program, attendance at a church service, and the median SAT score of applicants to a college. These are measures of productivity of certain efforts. The number of participating homes in a crime watch program is not an output equal to a statistical reduction of crime, but it is better than nothing. Church attendance might not be reflected in the lives of the congregation, but it measures a dimension of effort. The quality of college applicants is not necessarily relevant to the education they will receive, but it can be a measure.

But organizational leadership should resist the seductiveness of measuring the process rather than its results. It is temptingly satisfying to measure the height, breadth, and depth, the volume, velocity, and magnitude of efforts and activities while ignoring accomplishment and results. Writing in *Voluntary Agencies in the Welfare State*, Ralph Kramer notes a problem resulting from deficiencies in governmental monitoring of their funding of social services, stating that "there will be a tendency to simplify and to reduce standards to quantifiable terms, and that voluntary agencies will be judged by profit-making criteria."[28]

Activity is not the same as accomplishment, and effort is no substitute for results. A bicycle and a rocking chair can both consume activity and effort, but one ends where it begins, and the other can take you to the corner store and back. Jim Naughton, of Georgetown University, and I were discussing the temptation to measure processes rather than results.[29] He said that the way to get to the meaningful measurement is to ask, "So what?" each time data are presented. He suggested that with each answer, the question should be repeated. If there is a means of determining a significant measure, "So what?" will peel away layer after layer of intermediate information until you reach the core.

Attitudes and behavior may be measured by surveys, pre- and posttests, and expert evaluation techniques, such as the Delphi method. If objectives have been precisely defined, the results can be compared with the aspirations: Were you able to get the Legislature to pass the bill? Was the building finished on time at the budgeted cost? Is the cost per unit of service increasing or decreasing?

Since much of the output of voluntary enterprises concerns quality rather than quantity, the difficulty of qualitative measures must be emphasized. Often the quality of the service cannot be measured in any absolute way. However, the degree to which the recipients of the service perceive the quality can often be measured, and the quantitative response to the service in terms of demand should reflect its quality. Some type of professional or expert peer-review process can also be used to ascertain the quality of services. It achieves some degree of accountability in those areas where a high degree of professional judgment is required. For instance, within the medical field, the Professional Standard Review Organizations were established by federal law to provide a mechanism for assuring quality of care in Medicaid, Medicare, and Child Health services. In most states, an entity has been established for this purpose under the auspices of the state medical society. Among accountants we have the CPA; among secretaries, the CPS; among Chamber of Commerce executives, the CCE; and among insurance people, the CLU. To a lesser degree, the reputation an organization enjoys among similar organizations in the field is a rough measure of quality. The various rankings of graduate schools in major universities is a case in point of an attempt to develop a qualitative measure for degrees of excellence.

This brings us to two questions. First, if the alternatives available to a decision-maker are so close to each other as to be given serious consideration, are truly precise measures actually relevant? Second, is the cost of developing quantitative measures of the value of a service worth the results obtained?

In answer to the first question, measurements may not have to be precisely accurate or absolute in order to be useful for decision purposes. In the fields in which voluntary enterprises engage, precise accuracy is often extremely difficult, and if the rough measures involving two alternatives are so close that one might desire more precise measurements, would the choice of one alternative over the other be that critical? Therefore, crude and unorthodox measurements might be the best that can be obtained under the inevitability that there will be some error and inaccuracy in any measurement. Precision in measurement should not be sought for its own sake, but as a means to an end. However, when a decision is made on the basis of a rough measurement, it is more likely to be the right decision if it is made within a matrix of as many precise measurements as are feasible.

In answer to the second question, there are many cases when the cost of measurement will be greater than the cost of providing the service. Herbert Heaton, former comptroller of the Rockefeller Foundation, helped me conduct a not-for-profit management conference in 1982. He cited the problem of prison psychiatrists spending 90% of their time writing reports on the 10% of their time that they spend in perfunctory interviews with their "patients." Dr. Heaton also noted the problem of protective record keeping, which in some cases takes precedence over work. He gave an example of hospital tests unrelated to the patients' needs but designed to protect against malpractice suits. Another example is the case of schools using teachers for clerical duty, which built a record of apparent efficiency in administrative costs. The loss of teaching time was not as readily measured. Use effective and realistic methods. Install a cost-effective system rather than taking the foolish route of seeking measurement for the sake of measurement.

When absolute measures of output are not feasible, relative measures can, and often are, used. By this I refer to comparisons between organizations or across departments within an organization, historical measures of change between time units, or normative comparisons against an ideal. In the absence of absolute measures, relative measures can at least indicate trends.

In his book, *Productivity in Service Organizations*, Herbert Heaton wrote:

> Both profit and nonprofit organizations can measure productivity in terms of annual rates of change, which is the way cost of living is measured. Using subjective as well as objective measurements, not only overall productivity but changes in the separate elements of efficiency and effectiveness can be measured this way. *Measuring change* makes improvement the objective, gives support to processes of Developing and Achieving.[30]

Conclusion

Many voluntary enterprise managers feel "shut up in measureless content."[31] The market value of the services of voluntary enterprises are not as measurable as those of business. Many services remain in the voluntary sector for this reason. If the market value were more measurable and predictable, the service would likely be provided by a business. The difficulty in measurability, or the lack of it, presents many problems, especially in a time when more and more emphasis is placed on cost-effectiveness, management by objectives, and accountability.

Since the voluntary enterprise does not have a mandate to make a profit, it has relative freedom and flexibility. Lack of measurability is not the same as lack of worth. Voluntary enterprises work in many areas that in retrospect prove to be valuable, but that are not measurable in the short term. They are able to pioneer on society's cutting edge. But this can be a nightmare for the manager whose job is to make things happen in an environment prone to imprecision. The human-relations values so important in voluntary organizations give it another dimension in which process is given priority. This sector provides many societal values that will continue to be impossible or impracticable to measure. Also, the organizational outputs are often characterized by so many variables that the best of measurement can be misleading. Under pressure to measure something, many organizations make the mistake of measuring inputs rather than outputs, and this may create more problems than it solves. The difficulty of measurability can make goal attainment difficult and could inhibit management in its attempts to choose from among alternatives.

The manager should always work toward decreasing uncertainty and increasing the precision of measurement whenever it will increase effectiveness. But the leader must recognize that a degree of lack of measurability is endemic to voluntary enterprises. Overreaction to pressures to produce measurements could result in selecting the wrong items to measure. This can distort an organization's activities and adversely affect its purpose.

When measurement of outputs is difficult, some managers feel more comfortable by measuring their inputs or their processes. This can lead to distortions and incorrect conclusions, when they are deceived into viewing such as measurements of results.

Methods for measuring soft data are gradually being developed. Where practicable, they can be significant management tools. However, many effective decisions can be based on rough estimates, and there are cases in which the pursuit of exact measurement is not cost-effective.

4

DISTINCTIVE PURPOSES

One ship sails East, and another West
While the selfsame breezes blow.
It is the set of the sail
And not the gale
That bids them where to go.

Ella Wheeler Wilcox[32]

A distinctive characteristic of voluntary enterprises is that their purposes are other than profit-seeking. This does not mean that a voluntary enterprise does not have money. Some, like the Rockefeller Foundation, have greater financial resources than many corporations. But a distinctive feature is that their reason for being is not profit. Their purpose does not lie in producing goods or providing a service at a price greater than its cost to generate revenue for an owner or a stockholder. While the organization may be concerned about generating as much revenue as it can, the income itself is not the end purpose envisioned by the founders. Therefore, its objectives, values, results, and measures of success differ significantly from those of a business. It provides services for its constituency, or for society on behalf of its constituents.

Such voluntary enterprises fall into two categories. There are those specifically established for the benefit of their members, and those designed to meet a broader societal purpose. But whether it is expressive (for the participants), such as a fraternal lodge, a baseball team, or an artist's association, or instrumental (for society), such as a hospital, a university, or an orphanage—it was not established for the purpose of profit.

Expressive Organizations

Expressive organizations exist to meet affiliation needs. The organizations provide friendship, recreation, status, self-help, and opportunities for advancement and self-aggrandizement for their members and participants. Many have no formal structure and can exist indefinitely without need of bank account, incorporation, or staff. Others, such as the Masonic Lodge, are ancient in age and international in structure. Some might be as unpretentious as a ladies bridge club, others as grandiose as a New Orleans Mardi Gras krewe. The values of expressive organization members lie in such things as enjoyment, status, camaraderie, business interaction, or "the good life." Success is measured in terms of the quality of their members, the comfort and beauty of their property, the ability of the organization to provide information, status, or business or social contacts, or how well the organization stands in relation to competitive groups.

Winning the America's Cup every four years is of great value to the New York Yacht Club. The American Society of Industrial Engineers is doing well at establishing the professional status of its members. Having members who win fly-casting competitions might be a measure of success for the Pine Junction Anglers Club. Being the most sought after fraternity on the campus may be the major goal of the ΣAE chapter. None of these values is related necessarily to income. Expressive organizations must constantly work on integration (solidarity and cohesion among its membership and units) and reinforcing the integrity of its value system.

Instrumental Organizations

Instrumental organizations have value systems and success measures quite different from those of business. In most cases the "outputs" of instrumental organizations are measured in numbers of graduates, patients, or clients. The organizations put a heavy emphasis on their reputation, the kind and quality of the publicity they receive, the prestige of their staffs and board members, and the tally of their accomplishments. A premium is placed on having a popular, trendy, dramatic, or timely cause. The accounting system might be obsolete, the financial "float" might be bobbing like a cork in a choppy sea, yet the organization can still be considered successful. The measures of success can be too subjective to be evaluated by business standards.

For example, a *Wall Street Journal* editorial criticized the Columbia University History Department.[33] Using business values and business-oriented cost–benefit measures, the author unzipped his calculator and demonstrated his point. "Investing in a Ph.D. in some fields still makes good sense," he wrote: "Ph.D.'s in medical science, engineering or computer science, for example. On the other hand, Ph.D.'s in history, English literature or classics, have low or negative returns. . . ." He may have been right, but all of his calculations were based on his idea that education is for economic ends.

Few would agree today with Herbert Spencer, who said, "Education has as its object the formation of character."[34] But would anyone agree that the object of education is solely financial?

Instrumental organizations also have their expressive side. Members who voluntarily contribute time, money, or expertise might receive psychological and other satisfactions. In some organizations, the stated *instrumental* purpose is a well-intended guise for *expressive* activity. Minority groups have criticized the "ego-tripping" aspects of some social agencies, where poor people are used as the objects of agency activities without solicitation of the recipients' own perceptions of their needs.

Purpose: Business versus Voluntary Enterprise

Business enterprises have a common purpose, while the purposes of voluntary enterprises are varied. Business purpose is clear, up-front, unambiguous, and relatively simple: profit. In its development a business may forgo earnings in the interest of expansion or a greater share of the market. But it exists to create customers, to buy low and sell high, to make a profit, to provide a return on investment. The larger and more complex the business, the more it may concern itself with political, social, environmental, and community affairs, but its central purpose is still profit. Success in business is quite measurable, clear, and tangible: Goals, values, and measures of success are all tied to profit-seeking.

That is not to say that profit is bad. In a fair exchange, both buyer and seller benefit. Many good and necessary things of life are provided by individuals and corporations that make a profit. Food, shelter, clothing, communication, and transportation have been provided through business activities for centuries. Nonprofit groups have no corner on the good, the valuable, or the worthwhile, their monopoly is on the unmeasurable. So voluntary enterprises have purposes other than the making of a profit, and these goals are often multiple and complex, often vague and ambiguous.

The line between the two sectors is not inviolate. Although a business cannot own a nonprofit enterprise, a nonprofit enterprise can own a business. Trade associations of businesses are not for the direct profit of the associations. Every large corporation has nonprofit staff and service organizations within it. Businessmen serve on voluntary enterprise boards, work on committees, and contribute to fund drives. Voluntary enterprises provide educational, health, welfare, and other supportive services for business. Certain departments of voluntary enterprises can be isolated or "privatized" and can stand on their own feet financially. Government owns and operates businesses such as Amtrak and the TVA and has its own volunteer organizations such as 4-H clubs. But taken as a whole, voluntary enterprises are distinctive in that their overriding purpose is to provide services to achieve an end other than profit.

Levels of Organizational Pursuits

Kenneth E. Boulding identifies different levels of organizations.[35] The highest is the "transcendental" level. Organizations that reach this level most often are voluntary enterprises. He characterizes transcendental systems as being in pursuit of ultimate and perhaps illusive knowledge, truths, and aesthetics. Religious and philosophical orders are examples.

Few business enterprises restricted to the practical and immediate need to show a profit will reach the transcendental level. But Boulding points out that the level can be reached by business organizations with emphases on knowledge and values other than the profit motive. A research and development firm like Edison's Menlo Park, for example, formed for altruistic ideals, can be transcendental. George Bernard Shaw may have been thinking of individuals when he wrote, "You see things and you say 'why?' But I dream things that never were; and I say, 'why not?'"[36] But his words also apply to some organizations, transcendental ones that dream of things that never were.

History supports the notion stated by David Horton Smith:

> The heretics of both science and religion are seldom supported in their work directly and consciously by the business or government sector. Only through non-profit organizations and the support of the voluntary sector have the major change in our view of the super-natural and its relation to the natural tended to come about in the past.[37]

All art, science, and religion is the attempt to show that disparate elements contribute to a universal homogeneous whole. Heretics— seeing the unity in elements far too disparate for the majority—make the breakthroughs by convincing others in a dream of a goal. Some "heretics" are known and admired: Jesus, Einstein, Rodin, Mohammed, Edison, Beethoven, Oppenheimer, Picasso. But how heretical was the person who said first, to those who killed sheep for their hides, that the strands of wool could be spun into thread, that thread could be woven into cloth, that if nurtured the sheep could provide many coats instead of just one. A heretical dream must have inspired others to adopt it and to act to achieve it.

Why do so many voluntary organizations exist? Because they constitute the best means to meet certain expressive and instrumental needs. Recognition of the needs predate and transcend modern economic concerns.

Our first cooperatively organized efforts were at a subsistence level. Those who cooperated survived, and contributed progeny. Those who tried to go it alone did not. So our communal instincts developed and strengthened into social bonds. We are social animals with an inherited need to live and work together toward common ends. Family and clan groups are voluntary organizations. Towns and municipalities are no more than extensions of our communal instincts.

We enjoy voluntary activity and may immerse ourselves in it for its own expressive sake. We obviously enjoy playing games, some of which really have no purpose beyond the play itself. We extend these games into our social intercourse, reflecting the early-taught lesson that significant values lie in joining together in purposeful activity.

Then there are the pragmatic objectives of the organizations themselves. Human tragedy injures the society itself, whether it be an unwed mother, who will be taken in by Catholic Charities, or a devastated coastal community assisted by the Red Cross. Few individuals or corporations see themselves as responsible for maintaining the traditions and relics of the past, but they recognize a responsibility for supporting libraries, historical societies, and museums, which preserve ideas, values, and artifacts. Injustice to man gave birth to the abolitionist movement, and later to the Congress on Racial Equality. Injustice to animals spawned the Society for the Prevention of Cruelty to Animals. The prevalence of cancer and heart disease led to the forming of the American Cancer Society and the Heart Foundation. Would any of these organizations have been established if man's organizational motivation was based purely on profit-seeking?

As large corporations identify a sense of social responsibility, they often respond philanthropically. Some such activity is for public relations, some is based on a political or even a marketing motive. But much corporate good-citizenship is a reflection of genuine social concern on the part of managers who perceive needs just as do other members of society. And how is this concern expressed? Almost inevitably in a nonprofit format—either through the support of outside enterprises or by the creation of internal nonprofit efforts.

As corporations continue to grow and to transcend national boundaries, they become societies in themselves, with their own culture and value system. For example, IBM, which began as an American company, now operates in over 60 countries, deals in 40 or 50 currencies, and has employees that speak over 20 languages. As the growth continues, expressive and instrumental needs arise, and voluntary enterprises emerge within that business society. Some needs will be met by existing organizations, others by internal counterparts to existing agencies within the business itself.

Voluntary enterprises tend to be idealistic in their purposes. Their founders are often charismatic individuals with idealistic visions bordering on obsessions. Their dedication and commitment, plus their ability to call attention to the need and to demonstrate the validity of a program, elicited energy from the social environment sufficient to launch the organization.

These individuals often assemble a following that shares their intolerance for wrong. If Moses had tolerated slavery and not developed a following, there would have been no Exodus. If Jesus had been tolerant of an outmoded traditionalism and had not recruited his disciples, there would have been no Christianity. If Luther had quietly tolerated the sale of indulgences, there would have been no Reformation. If Washington had been tolerant of taxation without representation, there would have been no American Revolution. Human slavery, cannibalism, disease, poverty, ignorance—each practice has been challenged by one obsessed individual who gathered followers. Martin Luther King, Jr., said, "I have a dream." Others, through King, gave voice to a dream of their own by joining with him.

Many groups, at the other end of the scale, never got off the ground. Some exist in a limbo of lost causes. But few meander so far from their idealistic source that they completely lose touch. For it is that idealistic source that provides most of them with their power: the power to inspire, the power to elicit energy, in the form of voluntarily contributed time, money, and expertise. Some ideals are realizable; some are impossible—but there is power in striving to realize the most impossible of dreams.

I remember attending an annual meeting of the Explorers Club at the invitation of Lowell Thomas, to hear a speech by my friend Wendell Phillips. But my reason for remembering it so vividly was listening to another guest, a member of the Broadway cast of *Man of La Mancha*, who sang "The Impossible Dream." In that setting, among men who had climbed Everest, explored the depths of the sea, and mapped uncharted deserts and jungles, I would have signed up for anything when the song ended. There is great power in an idea, and even greater power when the idea is clothed in effective organization.

Occasionally, an entire society can get caught up in an idealistic cause. When an ideal or a social need transcends individual self-interest, even life can be forfeit: Witness Masada, the Alamo, Jonestown. For a large complex nation, such response to idealism is hard. But it can happen. As Peter Drucker reminds us in *Management:*

> Again and again, we find either a period or a particular organization in which working is achievement and fulfillment. The usual case is a great national emergency, in which the worker sees himself contributing to a cause. This happened, for instance, in Great Britain in the months after Dunkirk. On a smaller scale it occurred in the United States during World War II. Jobs did not change. Bosses did not become more intelligent or more humane. But the basic satisfaction of working changed completely, if only for a limited period.[38]

Advantages to Voluntary Enterprises

We have looked at some of the reasons why we have voluntary enterprises. Consider now some positive aspects that stem from their distinctive type of purpose.

Obviously, voluntary enterprises provide far-ranging purposes, something for everyone. Whether an individual feels strongly about an issue and seeks allies for amplifying efforts, or seeks satisfying comradeship around an interest, a vehicle exists.

Equally obvious are the channels voluntary enterprises provide for solving problems that are quite apart from financial gain.

I recently participated in a trade conference involving Latin American nations sponsored by the International Trade Mart in New Orleans. Hundreds of leaders from throughout the Western Hemisphere attended. The sponsoring organization only "made" $218 (the difference between income and costs). But in addition to the constructive business that was transacted, top-level leaders from two hostile Central American nations got together in a neutral environment and resolved some of their problems. If the motive had been profit, the conference would have been a failure.

Voluntary enterprise is a format well-suited to provide a means for the more fortunate to care for the less fortunate, and for both to help themselves. When any group of ranchers, minority groups, or employers needs to pursue a common economic or social goal, the organizations are ready. They were established to help individuals participate in pension funds and health insurance, to enable farmers to market their products more effectively, and to enable employers to form trade associations that would broaden their access to information. As Jon Van Til of Rutgers said to me: "The vision of voluntary enterprise is ultimately a vision of a just and humane society. We need to keep that vision alive by asking, 'What are the needs of society?' "

The voluntary sector provides a forum that encourages discussions of right and wrong, needed change, and altruistic concerns for the future. The groups are uniquely equipped to contribute toward the kind of world each of us wants, and to facilitate a striving toward change in a responsible, constructive, and purposeful manner. Within voluntary enterprises, citizens can identify persons of like mind to whom they can lawfully express their righteous indignation. The enterprises are instruments available as means for change.

Many voluntary enterprises have transcendental purposes. Working within their framework, an individual can help himself, the organization, and the society simultaneously while engaged in a single activity. In this sort of organization, what is good for the individual is good for the organization, and what is good for the organization is good for the individual. The experience is at Maslow's level of self-realization or self-actualization.[39] A lack of goal conflict is highly motivating to the individual and highly enriching to the society. The organization facilitates sociability, comradeship, and other expressive benefits. In so doing, it is an enriching, integrating factor for the society.

Disadvantages to Voluntary Enterprises

There are disadvantages in enterprises with a not-for-profit purpose. Many of the endemic problems will be discussed in later chapters. At this point I will mention a few general ones.

1. The original purpose is usually a goal of the finest caliber. But in setting up the mechanism for accomplishing the goal, good intentions can be thwarted. Organization is sensitive, like a plant that can wilt under the heat of a variety of adverse factors. Personal ambitions can confuse direction; the changing moods of society can dry up sources of support; the temptation of a new opportunity can divert an original course. An enterprise must be responsive to a variety of public pressures and must satisfy many needs at the same time.

2. Because the enterprises get their support from sources other than their clients, they are dependent on the other sectors. At the time that government or profit-seeking sectors are unable or unwilling to provide

resources, the demand for services could be at its apogee. This basic dependency can create real crisis. (Of course, the other sectors also depend on the voluntary sector, but usually this dependence is long-range and the cause-and-effect relationship not as obvious as is the need for financial support.)

3. Competition can be introduced from both of the other sectors. A voluntary enterprise that really does its job well might develop its own competition from the profit sector. When it founders, its role could be taken over by the public sector. For example, I worked with a voluntary enterprise in the early 1960s that did a good job of developing and publishing reading materials for adults with poor reading skills. They used a controlled vocabulary for a person with less than a fifth-grade reading ability, but the subject matter was of interest and use to adults. The enterprise was the only source providing the service, and there was a great need. It was a nonprofit operation because the readers were at the poverty level. Simultaneously, the organization was an advocate for more attention to the functionally illiterate.

Then came President Lyndon Johnson's War on Poverty. The organization's advocacy role had contributed to the new focus. Suddenly, vast sums of money became available. The private sector moved in, and major publishers put out highly attractive competing literature. It was material originally prepared for youth, but it sold at a profit. The government began its poverty program and competed from yet another angle. Though the not-for-profit organization did well, it had massive competition from sources that previously had shown little interest.

Nursing homes are another example. When Medicare was introduced, many private profit-seeking homes opened. Several large corporations entered the field. Today, both not-for-profit and profit-seeking homes compete with each other in the same communities.

4. The National Foundation for Infantile Paralysis with its "March of Dimes" labored long and well to fight polio. It won. Polio lost. So did the National Foundation. Its very success preempted its purpose. It did what no private enterprise could do—it reached its ultimate goal and had no place else to go. No one needed it anymore, which was wonderful for those threatened with polio and great for society. (It also benefited the private profit-seeking sector—the drug industry—by providing it with another product to sell at a profit.) But those who had achieved success were faced not with reward but with unemployment. The enterprise kept the personnel and the structure intact, modified its name, and found a new purpose—birth defects. It had been in business to work itself out of a job. It succeeded, then started again with a new purpose.

Implications for Leaders

The distinctive purposes of voluntary enterprises profoundly affect the setting of goals and objectives and the planning and evaluation functions. Purpose determines the organization necessary to ensure the commitment of persons whose activities are necessary to fulfill that purpose. The awareness of original goals would seem so self-evident that they need not even be mentioned. But as an organization grows older, urgent and pressing matters can divert its leaders' attention. Newcomers, anxious to be noticed, but ill-grounded in the organizational purpose, will have their say. Pressures from regulating bodies and funding sources have their influence. Well-meaning and persuasive persons, unfamiliar with not-for-profit management, can have their input. Many factors can divert the course of thinking. Regularly, there must be a recall to the organization's central reason for being.

The cost-effectiveness so central to business thinking does not necessarily transfer easily to the voluntary sector. It stresses cost-to-benefit ratio and economy. But beyond a certain point, such an emphasis can be counterproductive in an organization with a different value system—a system that stresses unmet needs, quality of service, attitudes, and the environment and quality of life.

The manager must keep organizational goals and values paramount. He must align the various components of the enterprise toward the achievement of its purpose and keep it contained within its value system. Since values are often an integral part of purpose, ends rarely justify means. Often the idealistic purposes of the organization are of a higher level than those of the individuals who do its work. On the one hand, this will tend to uplift the individuals and give them a focus for self-improvement. On the other hand, management must counteract a tendency to downgrade the purpose for more self-serving personal needs.

Many of the major contributors and board members will have a business orientation and a superficial understanding of what really makes the organization work. When this is linked with a disproportionate influence on policy, the manager can have serious problems. Unless the goals and value system are clearly defined, and stated in clear objectives, the business-oriented person can throw a monkey wrench into the gearbox. The possibility is another reason why the voluntary enterprise manager should understand the differences in management of the two sectors. If he has a clear understanding in his mind, he may be able to make it clear in the mind of the business-oriented contributor or board member.

I had a long talk with Congresswoman Lindy Boggs on this problem. She was familiar with the tendency of a businessman to assume
that the bank balance could measure not only the effectiveness of a
voluntary enterprise but also the effectiveness of government agencies.
Having served on the congressional Post Office Committee, she cited a
history of problems that grew out of misconceptions concerning the
purpose of the postal service. "Its main objective was to get the mail
delivered through hail and snow and the threat of the dark of night."
Through a series of changes, services have deteriorated significantly.
She said, "The feeling of urgency and the protectiveness of the personal
aspect of the citizens has diminished, and mail service certainly has been
diluted."[40]

When government gets involved either as a regulator or as a funding source, purpose can be affected. This is especially true of organizations with purposes that are critical of government. Large infusions of
government funds tend to "turn off" volunteer board members, according to Jon Van Til, former president of the Association of Voluntary
Action Scholars.[41] When I asked him what he meant, he replied: "They
concentrate on the non-government-funded aspects of the organization.
They worry about who should be in what staff position or whether the
financial report is in order. Boards simply do not choose to address
questions as to what the federal funds are doing in the organization."
On the other hand, Van Til says that the big gainer from the infusion of
government funds is the chief executive officer.

In terms of goals and objectives, the management might also have
to contend with a conflict between the primary organizational goals and
the expressive goals of volunteers. Ideally, the two needs should be
aligned, but one can inhibit the other. Management has more control
over expressive goals of staff members, since they control administrative
incentives and sanctions. There can also be a conflict between their own
goals and those of the organization.

In the staffing function, management must utilize organizational
purpose to recruit volunteers, build conviction, elicit energy from them,
and inspire them to their best effort. They must develop means for
bonding and building a sense of cohesion among the constituency and
staff around the purpose and goals. This is why a charismatic management style can be so effective.

The service nature of voluntary enterprises is a management consideration. Once, not-for-profit enterprises provided material goods; today, they deal almost exclusively with services. Even when goods are
involved, close inspection will usually show that the organization's
function is the service of *delivering* the material goods. Service organiza-

tions are at the opposite end of the spectrum from manufacturing, which utilizes precise measurements and predictability. In service organizations, for instance, a line cannot easily be drawn between administrative costs and the cost of providing the service. The marketing of services is not as well developed as the marketing of hard goods.

In planning, the definition of purpose and the writing of goals and objectives is of critical importance. Evaluating the productivity of the enterprise in relation to its purpose is of paramount consideration. There is a subtle but essential difference here. In contrast to a business, a not-for-profit group's whole reason for being can be embodied in such statements. In business, the financial *bottom line* is the reason for being, and the statements tend to be strategy arguments concerning means.

Herbert Heaton notes that the concept of accountability is widely applied in business and often misunderstood in nonprofit organizations. He wrote:

> To be answerable for what one does, one must first have objectives outside oneself, and we have seen that these are lacking in non-profit hierarchies of authority. Too often the thrust in non-profit organizations has been to deny not only commercial purpose or practicality, but any purpose of any kind. To improve the productivity of any organization, there must be unrelenting pressure for purpose, accountability, and responsibility.[42]

Charismatic personalities are often drawn to the voluntary sector because of the nature of the organizations and their purposes. Etzioni points out that commitment and identification of followers to their leaders is the major means by which values are created, transmitted, or extended. He writes:

> Communication studies demonstrate the low effectiveness of formal communication not supported by informal leaders, and the importance of positive affective interpersonal relations between the priest and the parishioner, the teacher and the student, the political leader and his followers, for effective operation of their respective organizations . . . in short, the attainment of culture goals such as the creation, application, or transmission of values requires the development of identification with the organizational representatives.[43]

Such persons often have ego needs greater than their needs for financial rewards. On the positive side, the organization and the individual both get what they want. On the negative side, the individual's ego needs can be difficult for other *capable* persons to live with, and those needs can conflict with what is best for the enterprise itself.

The board members are affected by the purpose. They obviously would not serve without compensation were it a profit-seeking entity. Working within the framework, the organization should attract an optimum board through an attractive mix of enticements, including a worthy purpose, an appealing image, and appropriate recognition and appreciation.

In attracting staff, the not-for-profit purpose plays a part. Generally, the group requires dedicated individuals with the competency required for their assigned tasks. Often persons respond to a purpose that coincides with their ideals, and the tasks and recognition give them personal satisfaction and fulfill their need to serve. They tend to be people-oriented, and have a relatively low need for being able to measure their progress in a tangible way.

Without resources in the form of contributions and workers, there would be no organization. Without an appealing purpose, there would be no voluntarily contributed resources. So here, too, management should be concerned with a clear purpose, attractively exposed to sources of resources. This is often difficult to separate from the image projected by the organization's personnel: its founder, its chief executive, its board members, the staff and volunteers. The clients or members, depending on the nature of the enterprise, are the beneficiaries of the organization's purpose. The flow of benefits in a nonprofit organization is from the contributors, through the organization, and to the clients. In a profit-seeking organization, the purpose is to have the flow of major benefits in the opposite direction—toward the providers of capital.

Motivation of both paid and unpaid workers is linked to the purpose. This can be difficult in functions far removed from the service delivery point. But the wise manager will tie all facets of the enterprise to its ultimate purpose and utilize it as a motivation.

I remember the deluge of letters I got each spring from students offering their services when I was the chief executive of an international voluntary organization. This is not a business executive's kind of experience. The letters were inspiring in their enthusiasm, idealism, and response to our cause. But they were so much alike as to have used the same outline, year in and year out. After explaining how they had learned about us, and what their personal aims were, they offered themselves free for a full summer's work. Then there was the afterthought— always in the final paragraph—they wanted the exotic face-to-face dealing with the recipients of our services. Each made it clear that he didn't want to spend the summer running a mimeograph.

Since I doubt that we had a mimeograph in any of our offices, they would be spared that fate. (Somewhere there must have been an agency with acres of mimeographs, each manned by summer volunteers, who—when they returned to school in the fall—were handed my name and address.) The point is to so structure the objectives that each cog in the machine knows the contribution it makes to the ultimate purpose.

The same holds true in the feedback system for controlling the work and evaluating progress toward goals. There should be some obvious degree of progress toward achieving the organization's purpose.

Conclusion

Ends that require organized effort and for which measurement of market value is difficult are achieved through not-for-profit organizations. Though the ultimate recipient of the services of the organization and its volunteer leadership pursue the fulfillment of different needs, the enterprise has a purpose other than profit as its reason for being. Such organizations enrich the quality of life of individuals, provide many important purposes for society, and achieve many worthwhile goals. Their purposes are perceived as important enough to elicit a significant amount of energy in the form of voluntarily contributed time, money, and expertise.

Voluntary enterprise activities may be quite similar to their profit-seeking or government-sector counterparts, but it is the purpose that makes them significant. For instance, I visited Albert Schweitzer at his jungle hospital in Gabon a few days before he died. I saw an institution with a management approach quite different from that of the government hospital a few miles away in the town across the river. Schweitzer's hospital was relatively ill-equipped, but overflowing with patients and their families. The government hospital appeared bureaucratic and was relatively empty. And both institutions in Gabon were far different from Herman Tarnower's Scarsdale Medical Center, where I had my annual checkup. All three clinics were in the healing business, but the effectiveness of each would be measured by a different yardstick.

Voluntary enterprises take a different path. Those who lead down that path must have different skills.

5

THE VOLUNTEER TOOL

"You can't imagine what it's like," says the businessman to the voluntary enterprise manager.

"What do you mean?" the manager responds.

"Unless you've had to meet a payroll out in the real world of business, you can't imagine what it's like!"

"I have to meet a payroll too."

"Yes, but it's not the same! In your kind of organization it's not as rough and tumble. It's just not the same!"

"I see what you mean. I have to motivate most of my people to work for free, and on top of that, to pay for effort I can't get for free I have to get people to give us money to meet our payroll. You are right. It is not the same!"

It is not the same! Since no individual owner or stockholder makes a profit, and the organization has a not-for-profit purpose, people will pitch in and help. Voluntarily contributed energy in the form of resources such as time, money, and expertise is the special tool of the voluntary sector. Whether the organization is labor-intensive, like the Junior League, or capital-intensive, like an art museum, someone has been willing—without coercion or promise of repayment in kind—to help achieve its purpose. Voluntarily contributed resources are its chief means of doing its work.

Government, on the other hand, utilizes the rule of law implemented by implied or enforced coercive powers to fulfill its purpose. The state has a monopoly, and compliance is relatively unavoidable. The law prescribes standards of conduct and exacts penalties for nonconformance with unique sanctions and powers. Whether the state is totalitarian (without the consent of the majority of those governed) or democratic (by their consent), the state does not rely on voluntarism to do its job. Operating within the rule of law is unavoidable, unless you choose an antisociety outlaw existence. Government is a means of achieving a number of important ends.

Business uses the principle of exchange in the marketplace to produce a profit. Whether it does well at the exchange process or not, its economy is based on providing goods or services to parties who give back something in exchange. Since its purpose is to accomplish the trade so that it ends up with a surplus, voluntary contributions of goods or services have no part in the process. Adam Smith said, "Man is an animal that makes bargains: no other animal does this—no dog exchanges bones with another."[44] Barter, or exchange, is an excellent tool with which an honest seller and a willing buyer can arrive at a mutually beneficial arrangement. The market mechanism is a means by which we achieve many of our ends. The mechanism provides the right of individual choice to secure a variety of goods and services.

In the voluntary sector, objectives are achieved through voluntary action. The volunteer contributor or worker is neither coerced nor paid to provide efforts. They are, as Tracy Connors wrote, "the vehicles by means of which people pursue together goals that are not primarily remunerative and that they are not forced to pursue."[45] Since voluntary enterprises operate on an altruistic-income economy having neither the power of taxation (coercive-income economy) nor goods to exchange in a market economy, they must rely on persuasion to elicit resources. The resources include the giving of time: time to solicit gifts, time to serve clients, time to stuff envelopes, time to attend meetings, time to make phone calls. It includes the voluntary contribution of money, securities, real estate, food, and other goods. It includes expertise: A businessman, politician, or professional person might contribute expertise for which he would otherwise be paid.

In apposition to this model are those who see voluntarism also working in an economy of exchange. For their time and money they receive intangible benefits. Among these are such things as satisfaction, a feeling of well-being, a clear conscience, a sense of participation, camaraderie, recreation, honor, and recognition. The benefits are directly related to communal instincts. Leaders in the voluntary sector use the exchange awareness as a motivator in seeking organizational resources. Some of the same intangibles are gained by compliance with the law, or for exchange in a market economy. But for our purposes: *Voluntarism, produced by persuasion, is the principal tool of voluntary enterprises.* It is unavailable to the other sectors, and any exchange is largely of an intangible and subjective nature.

Government in a democracy seeks to maximize its values to the public within a given set of resources, or to minimize the cost of providing a fixed amount of service. A profit-seeking enterprise seeks to optimize profit and minimize costs, subject to the constraints of society.

Voluntary enterprises seek to elicit a maximum amount of energy and manage it effectively in pursuit of the goals of its constituency.

Why is voluntarism produced by persuasion the chief tool of organizations? From a negative point of view you can say it is the only thing left. The nature of such groups is such that they cannot survive on exchange when the market value of their outputs is relatively unmeasurable and—by definition—they have no coercive power. All that is left is what they can get people to contribute. Some organizations in this sector, such as foundations, operate as best they can without seeking contributions of time and money at all. Once they are capitalized, they operate on exchange. Perhaps voluntarism was a starting point, but the tool has long since been developed, modified, and refined into a complex implement.

Voluntarism is a positive good, not a last resort. Entire organizations are established to satisfy expressive needs and to provide opportunities for the exercise of voluntarism. A good case can be made for voluntary action as an autonomous experience of human life.

David S. Adams compared voluntary action to activities such as work, play, and love, and says that it should be comprehended as a distinct mode of behavior. "It is action which is an end in itself."[46] He continues: "Voluntary action is fun. . . . The undeniable fun of voluntary action seems to me to be a characteristic of this phenomenon almost entirely overlooked in the literature." He summarizes his response to the question "What sort of phenomenon is voluntary action?" by suggesting the following points:

1. Voluntary action, like play, is a legitimate existential category for humans. It is experienced by those who engage in it as a type of action which is different from all other types of action.
2. Voluntary action, like play, is an end in itself. Voluntary associations are often goal-directed social groups; the voluntary act is, in itself, its own end. Like play, it is fun.
3. Voluntary action, like play, is freely performed. In common with much human action it is norm-governed, but voluntary action differs from other forms of human action because in it the actor freely agrees to follow its norms. Voluntary acts are voluntarily performed.

This is part of the expressive aspect of voluntary enterprises. If it is natural for people to volunteer, a very positive value exists in organizations designed to facilitate that desire.

Work also is an autonomous human activity. It is planned and accomplished to achieve a purpose. So when a person undertakes voluntary action in the form of work, regardless of whether or not he enjoys it, it is for an instrumental end. Regardless of whether we classify the organization as expressive (to meet the needs of members) or instrumental (for some societal purpose), the individual can have both motivations personally. When someone is attracted to an organization by its instrumental objectives, and finds self-expression and fulfillment in the contribution he makes, he is engaged in a multirewarding activity. This is another reason why the benefit of voluntary action is so great and why it can be such a significant tool. As Richard Cornuelle and Robert Finch wrote, "Nothing can melt human and social problems faster than the willingness of one individual to involve himself voluntarily in helping another individual overcome his problem."[47]

Persuasion is the means used by voluntary enterprises to instill a desire within potential contributors of time and money. It either overcomes inertia on the part of a dormant prospect and attracts him or it converts energies that otherwise would be used elsewhere. Or, if you wish, it exposes the volunteer worker or contributor, who is looking for a vehicle, to the virtues of a particular organization. The case made by the persuader seeking to recruit workers may appeal to several motivations. It may simply point to the end to be achieved ("cure crippled children"). Or it may appeal to the individual's self-interest ("a safer neighborhood"), provide expressive ends ("you'll meet a wonderful bunch"), or present a stepping-stone ("excellent experience"). Financial contributors will be shown tax advantages, cost-effectiveness, prestige, and how to get the "biggest bang for the buck." Whether low-key or high-pressure, persuasion is the means to secure a commitment for some form of resource.

Voluntary enterprises have used persuasion from the very beginning. I can easily visualize the members of a hunting band beckoning and grunting, trying to recruit a burly newcomer to join them in tracking a mastodon. "Evangelism" is a theme in the New Testament. Professional public relations specialists were seeking favorable comment in the press in Benjamin Franklin's day.[48]

So persuasion to produce voluntarily contributed resources has a long and well-justified place as a distinguishing feature in these organizations. Through persuasion so many do so much for themselves while helping so many others.

Aspects of Voluntarism

Examine now some of the positive facets of voluntarism as a means of getting things done. Five of the more attractive are the following:

1. It provides an automatic inward and outward flow of human relationships with its community.
2. It can elicit, store, and channel vast quantities of latent energy.
3. The quality of resources tapped through voluntarism can be disproportionally better than that tapped by other means.
4. It provides the capacity for stretching a small amount of seed money and a modest cadre of paid staff into a large amount of achievement.
5. It encourages the highest motives among those involved, and provides positive societal values.

The automatic flow of relationships develops a healthy interchange. Unless the organization is an isolated residential community or commune, there is an ebb and flow of financial and human resources between the enterprise and its encompassing society. If it has a wholesome relationship with its volunteer workers and contributors, the ebb and flow provides good word-of-mouth relations for the organization and automatically feeds into the organization the attitudes, expectations, and concerns of the community. The two keep in touch, encouraging an atmosphere of relevancy and realism. The built-in openness also provides feedback, and it can be a self-correcting mechanism when things go awry. Studies show that voluntary enterprises have more community involvement than commercial enterprises. The interchange is one reason why it is true.

The vast reserve of energy that voluntarism can elicit, store, and release to accomplish desired ends is perhaps the greatest asset of any enterprise. An emergency or a great idea provides dramatic evidence of this energy. I remember, for example, when I was a teenager and the Mississippi River threatened to overflow its banks, thousands of people responded to a call for help. They worked around the clock, some with shovels and sandbags, others with bulldozers. Lines of race, age, and status vanished in a massive (and successful) effort to shore up the bank. When the defeated British army was facing annihilation on the beach at Dunkirk, a fleet of volunteer English boatmen transferred their countrymen, in the face of an approaching German army, to their island homeland. Consider what a tiny organization with meager funds started in Montgomery, Alabama, when Rosa Parks wouldn't move to the back of the bus. A Baptist preacher said it was time other customers stopped riding buses if they could not sit where they wanted. Voluntarism did what neither government had accomplished nor business had attempted.

Voluntarism can provide resources of quality that would not be possible under comparable circumstances in the other sectors. Like a small child lifted to drink at a too-high water fountain by a strong man pausing on his hurried way, a voluntary enterprise can grasp beyond its reach. There are times when a telephone call from a powerful person, a facility provided for a day's meeting, an hour's consultation with an expert, or the loan of a signature on a letter can give an organization benefits it could not normally afford. Persons from all walks of life will give talents to an endeavor in a way that they would never do for pay.

The existence of voluntary action can vastly stretch the staff and treasury. In the case of informal coalitions and short-term efforts, much can be done with no staff at all and no pooling of funds. But most organizations operate in a routine between peaks of activity with a relatively small cadre of paid workers and a maintenance-level bank account. When a major annual campaign, the big exhibit, a seasonal high demand on services, or a catastrophe strikes, it expands like an accordion. For example, a trade association builds all year toward its annual convention and trade show. As the annual event approaches, the activities of the membership grow rapidly, then expand dramatically the week of the event itself.

Idealism pervades most voluntary enterprises. Idealism provides management challenges as well as opportunities. The interlarding of paid staff with volunteers and the dependence on contributed funds keep the organization close to its idealistic purposes. When a paid secretary, bookkeeper, or specialist is exposed to nonpaid idealistic volunteers, the idealism will often "rub off" on them. Initially, they may have chosen their jobs from among others on a pragmatic basis. But how can a secretary dawdle at her work when a person who is not being paid at all is working with her? The organization's ability to elicit voluntary action is directly proportionate to its ability to return a sense of relevancy value and satisfaction. As it changes and evolves over the years, voluntarism is an incentive toward a perpetuation of idealism. Even when an enterprise has purposes counter to its cultural context, it tends to embody the higher standards, values, and aspirations of its component groups. If it did not, it could not attract financial contributions and other forms of energy from its constituency. Its ideals enhance its ability to elicit voluntary action, which, in turn, tends to perpetuate the idealism.

One vital dimension of voluntary action is that some acts of service are valuable primarily because the service is unpaid and is seen as unpaid by the recipient. For example, a well-to-do professional who voluntarily teaches an unemployed illiterate how to read will get a better response than if the teacher were paid for his time. The learning process is lubricated by mutual respect and sincerity.

Part of this idealism in a democratic society is the interplay among persons of different racial and ethnic backgrounds, socioeconomic levels, and generational and vocational differences. A postman might sit on a United Way board with a corporate president. An independent shopkeeper and a lawyer could work together on a Big Brothers project. A widow on Social Security might get to know a young insurance salesman by working with him at church. This socialization process enriches the culture and exposes elements of society to each other in ways not otherwise possible.

Negative Aspects of Voluntarism

The negative facets, in the eyes of those with a business approach to organization, overshadow the brightness of the positive aspects. Indeed, if the organization does not take advantage of the benefits of voluntarism, the negatives can make the total picture appear dark. This is especially true with values oriented to task accomplishment, and with little concern for human relationships. The assets of voluntarism bring liabilities, such as softness, inefficiency, and sluggish response to direction.

The most obvious negative is that volunteers are not paid and contributors do not receive a direct return on their investment. Because volunteer workers are not paid, direct-line accountability is difficult to enforce. It can be achieved, but only by consent. It takes time and the development of an organizational culture in which accountability is accorded a high value. (The extreme adverse example of how individuals vest their leaders with power over their behavior is the Jonestown community. They gave sufficient power to Jim Jones that he could induce them to commit mass suicide. While such a degree of obedience is greater than that which financial incentives can achieve, it is not the norm for voluntary enterprises.) Normally, accountability is not directly enforceable. Often, volunteers gravitate to certain tasks, leaving the more difficult and less rewarding and satisfying jobs undone. Likewise, contributors are generally easier to get for the more glamorous, more visible short-term projects, leaving few resources for other projects that could have more strategic value.

It is often difficult to achieve selectivity over volunteers. You may have more than you can utilize at a time of low need, and none during an emergency period. You may not locate the talents you need at one point, and have a surplus at another. You may have the incompetent and counterproductive thrust upon you along with the excellent. And if

you attempt greater selectivity and an individual with influence is of-
fended, the resultant waves could threaten to swamp the boat. A survey
of businessmen revealed some of their frustrations in dealing with voluntary organizations. Seventy percent felt: "It means dealing with inca-
pable volunteers who slow down accomplishment and can't be fired."
Similarly, 61% complained: "Everything moves slowly compared to
business. Time is wasted." Slightly over half recognized: "It is difficult
to provide leadership for groups or committees of different kinds of
people trying to work together."[49]

Some writers claim that there is a diminishing interest in volunteering. Writing in *Psychology Today*, DeMott[50] quotes several leaders:

> Rev. Donald Larsen, executive director of the Lutheran Council of the United
> States, told me bluntly that recruiting is now a serious problem and getting
> more so. Shirley Leviton, chairwoman of the National Council of Jewish
> Women's Task Force on New Perspectives, sees voluntarism as definitely
> facing a bad time. "There are still some idealists around," says Mrs. Leviton,
> "but only some. People seem to be after instant gratification. What's in it for
> me? I'll do a service, maybe I'll give some time—but what do I get out of it?"

Fifty-one percent of Americans get a lot out of it.[51]

The intermittent or part-time nature of voluntary action also presents difficulties. While he or she may be dedicated to the cause and
derive much personal satisfaction from organization activity, a volunteer
usually has other overriding priorities. A youth has educational or pa-
rental priorities. Adults have livelihood and family considerations.
Older adults continue with family and health concerns. So their voluntary action is subject to both unexpected interruption and intervening
personal responsibilities. The problem is compounded by the democratic process of committee work. Getting key persons or a full committee together for six hours may take three weeks instead of one day. Not
only is the quantity of time they can commit less than if they were paid,
but the scheduling of the amount available is subject to other priorities.

Because of other priorities, the competition of volunteer opportunities, and the election of individuals to new positions, the volunteer
force is constantly changing. Recruits are unfamiliar with procedures,
interpersonal relations must be established, and objectives must be rein-
terpreted. Max Wortman[52] reminds us that the right and duties of position incumbents change as the individuals interact with their positions.
While this living, changing milieu has human relations assets, it can be a
liability in seeking to get a job done.

The greatest persuasive force can be the fact that the organization is
expressive as well as instrumental. It seeks to accomplish certain goals—
but it is also a community. As a community, the organizational norms

exert a strong persuasive normative influence over the adherents. As Etzioni's study notes:

> Normative organizations are organizations in which normative power is the major source of control over most lower participants, whose orientation to the organization is characterized by high commitment. Compliance in normative organizations rests principally on internalization of directives accepted as legitimate. Leadership, rituals, manipulation of social and prestige symbols, and resocialization are among the more important techniques of control used.[53]

Management Implications

In the planning function, efforts should be made to reduce uncertainty in the response of volunteers (and contributors) to any change. One program will "turn on" workers, who will work harder and more often than for another program. The difference could have little to do with which project provides more benefits to the organization. The more the enterprise depends on voluntary response, the greater the need for assessing the amount of energy that will be generated. Marketing is an internal as well as an external function.

When management begins to organize the system for accomplishing the task, you have both paid-staff and volunteer-staff components. Consideration must be given to coordinating one with the other. Since paid and unpaid persons work for different reasons, in different time frames, for different incentives, and in different supervisory modes and with different enforcement mechanisms, you cannot organize them in the same way. Also, once the organization's structure is designed, you should secure to a certain degree the consent of those who will work within it.

According to Kramer, whose study of social service organizations covered four countries, "It is widely held that there is an inherent conflict between professionalism and volunteerism."[54] My own experience does not bear this out when the full spectrum of the voluntary sector is considered. However, I have observed such an attitude in some instances. Perhaps it is more prevalent in organizations in which the professionals are primarily social workers, such as those in Kramer's study. He notes:

> Professionals have been described as the "full-time planners of other people's short-term bursts of energy and masochism." In practice, however, the situation is more complex, and an appropriate functional separation between paid staff and volunteers is a controversial issue. The generally accepted

view seems to be that if volunteers are used, they should extend or complement the work of paid staff, rather than substitute for it or threaten professionals' livelihood.[55]

When working with a project that depends for its success on a
major component of volunteer energy, I recommend redundancy techniques. Redundancy compensates for the unpredictability, inefficiency,
and lack of hard-nosed accountability when working with volunteers.
For instance, consider a goal to have 2,500 members of an association
attend five regional meetings. I would seek to have each region adopt an
attendance goal of, say, 700 instead of 500. We would then not have to
depend on each region meeting its goal to reach national figures. I
would have a national committee encouraging attendance through a
mailing list, a regional attendance committee working with individual
chapters, and perhaps a corporate committee working through the major employers of the organization members. If any of three attendance
efforts fails, the others would carry the load. If all succeed, we sell out
early.

In staffing, you must fill both paid and nonpaid positions. Often
you have to choose whether a job is done by a staff member or is
assigned to volunteers. You must be skilled in the subtleties of staff
reporting to volunteer committees, and vice versa. Volunteer recruiting
may require a special staff to keep all positions filled. Because of turn-
over and the sheer numbers with which you deal, training assumes a
major role. Through the entire process, volunteers should be instilled
with the conviction that the purposes of the organization are worth their
best efforts.

Eva Schindler-Rainman, who has consulted and written extensively
in the field of voluntarism, noted a number of current trends in the field
during a seminar we conducted (for more details, see Connors[56]):

1. New motivations are emerging.
2. More people from a greater variety of life-styles and backgrounds are volunteering.
3. New spaces and places and kinds of jobs for volunteers have
   become available.
4. The volunteer is demanding new conditions for the relationship
   between volunteer and agency.
5. Pressure is growing for increased collaboration between sectors
   of the world of voluntarism, on both national and local levels,
   and to some extent on the state level.
6. An increasing number of confrontations are occurring in the vol-

unteer world because of the rapid growth and visibility of voluntarism.

7. Pressure is increasing for new kinds of funding and new methods of accountability.
8. Legislative intervention bills are being introduced.
9. A new search for meaning is under way.

The management function traditionally designated "directing" is more properly called "guiding" when working with voluntary leadership and rank and file. Often you will have two complete systems, one for paid staff, who will accept more direct accountability and supervision and who often have longer-term motivations, and another for volunteers.

Tensions between volunteers and staff and among volunteers cannot be handled as easily as in a business organization. Relative status is often difficult to define. For instance, Ann, the college-educated wife of a $100,000-a-year business and civic leader, might volunteer to be part of a group that will canvass a neighborhood. How accurately they identify the number of senior adults will influence the job security of a 24-year-old social worker named John. When wearing another hat, Ann sits on the organization's board. Will she see her canvassing job as an assignment that properly requires her to work under the supervision of John? Will he make accommodations for her status in another relationship? What if a grant from the company of Ann's husband is paying for the whole project? What if she takes an out-of-town trip at a crucial time without notification? Does John replace her, do the job himself, or expect her to double up when she returns? Such conditions are commonplace and must be considered in monitoring volunteer performance.

Procedures for resolving conflict and differences of opinion should be established. Grievance procedures, similar to those in business and industry, are useful for paid staff. But the process among volunteers and between volunteers and staff requires other techniques. Cohesion is extremely important in such organizations. Occasions often arise when keeping the system together takes precedence over objectives, and goals are forfeit. Trade-offs between human-relations values and task values must be resolved. The guiding function in a voluntary enterprise is as much an art as it is a science, and it places heavy demands on voluntary enterprise managers at all levels.

In the control function, special problems can arise in enforcing performance standards. As the distance from highly accountable paid leadership increases, enforcement and accuracy of feedback at other levels decrease. Control is also difficult when management has meager financial rewards to offer its staff, and limited tools for discipline. With volunteers, the reward system is primarily operative in the process of doing work itself. A system of nonfinancial compensation must be established.

Conclusion

Voluntary enterprises do not have the coercive power of government, and their purposes limit their use of exchange in the marketplace. But they do have access to a great amount of energy through voluntarily contributed time, money, and other resources. This energy can be elicited, stored, and channeled by an enterprise with a compelling purpose and good management. Voluntarism, produced by persuasion, is the principal tool of organizations in this sector.

Voluntarism profoundly influences the organization's internal culture and the way it achieves its objectives. Because of reliance on this tool, if a voluntary organization is to thrive and survive, it must attract a constituency.

Both the positive and negative aspects of voluntary action in the form of volunteer workers and contributed income influence management strategy. To deal with volunteers and solicit contributions, special systems must be developed. The management of volunteers and the utilization of contributed resources produce special opportunities and problems. Such management functions as planning, organizing, staffing, guiding, and controlling are affected, and a great deal of coordination between staff and volunteers is required.

6

DUAL INTERNAL SYSTEMS

A hook-and-ladder fire truck has two steering wheels. The one in the cab is much like that in any other vehicle. The driver sees a pothole in the street, turns the steering wheel to avoid it, and the front wheels respond. The second steering wheel is manned by another driver perched high atop the tail end of the long truck. With it, he steers the back wheels. Without such an arrangement, the truck could not maneuver around corners. Working in tandem, the two hook-and-ladder drivers operate an effective apparatus for fighting fires and saving lives. Out of balance, they provide a spectacle fit for a Mack Sennett comedy.

The unique steering mechanisms of a hook-and-ladder truck are like many voluntary enterprises. For unlike a business enterprise with its single system, a voluntary enterprise has two relatively independent subsystems. Ideally, they work harmoniously in tandem, but the linkage between the two is far from automatic.

In voluntary enterprises, the development of resources and the providing of services are two distinct systems, while in business the two functions are integrated. In most not-for-profit enterprises, services are provided to clients who pay little or nothing toward the cost of those services. For example, Meals on Wheels provides food for persons in their homes, but funds for operating the service are provided by another source. A restaurant, in contrast, sells food and receives funds from the recipient for operating the service. The recipients might not even be identifiable: Society, as a whole, could be the recipient, as in the case of an organization dedicated to cleaning up the environment. Resources are provided by a system distinct from the service-providing systems. In contrast, business activity provides goods or services that produce revenue directly.

This difference is obvious in many of the day-to-day activities of a voluntary enterprise, yet it is too often overlooked in planning and evaluation at the management and policy levels.

The objectives of the service-providing system are the purposes for which the organization exists: to teach, heal, advocate, help, preach, entertain, persuade, or whatever. In fighting a fire, this is the system that directs the hose. Since the market value of the service is hard to measure, the individuals or segments of the population affected do not pay for this service directly. Scouts buy their uniforms, but they don't pay the full cost of being a Scout. A citizen watches a parade but doesn't pay for the band. A runaway child is given free food and shelter. The Society for the Prevention of Cruelty to Animals looks out for the welfare of animals, and environmental groups work for clean air. But neither the animals nor the air pay for the service.

Payment is provided by donors. In fighting the fire, donors are the fireplugs with their supply of water. Whether they are part of an established donor constituency or one-time givers among the general public, they are not paying directly an exact share of the service. They learn of the need for funds by word of mouth, through the mass media, in the mail, or from some sort of personal solicitation. The system that tells them of the need and provides a channel for receiving and transmitting the donation to the appropriate bank account is a second subsystem in the overall entity.

A business transaction, in contrast, symbolizes the single-system unity of profit-seeking enterprise. In the exchange between a buyer and a seller, you have the far end of the business cycle. All the efforts of manufacturing, sales, support groups, management, and labor are represented by what is sold. In return, the buyer pays a price. The amount paid is fed into the system, working its way back to begin a new cycle. The individuals receiving the goods or services pay for them. What they pay provides the resources for repeating the process.

For example, my wife and I operate a Texas ranch. We buy a quantity of Santa Gertrudis cattle. We improve the land, care for and occasionally provide extra food for the cattle. The cattle reproduce. We round up the calves and ship them to market. The cost of production is less than the price received. We use part of the profit to live on, part to improve the ranch, and part to care for the stock and perhaps buy replacement cattle for the next cycle. The cyclical process feeds on itself. The output of one cycle provides the input for the next.

The two types of organizations may be diagrammed as shown in Figure 1.

In the unified system of business, the sale of goods and services produces revenue directly. Organizational energy is converted to money at the point of sale, and new energy is injected back into the business. In the dual system of voluntary enterprise, one system provides the reve-

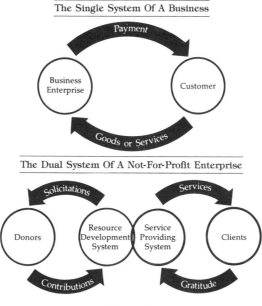

Figure 1

nue, while the other provides the service. We would like to think that when a service is provided, the grateful recipients or onlookers tell others about it. Hearing about the good work, generous contributors seek out the organization providing the service, and compensate the group for its efforts. In practice, energy must be spent in telling about the good done in order to elicit the resources. Hence, you have two independently functioning systems, each linked to the other within the organization.

Ideally, a relatively small portion of the organization's resources are required to tell about the need and what the organization can do about it with a given amount of money. The service provided and the resources contributed are in direct proportion to one another. Like the hook-and-ladder fire truck, the two systems can work well in tandem, one tracking behind the other. But this is not necessarily the case.

To illustrate the two-system nature of voluntary enterprises, consider the Jerry Lewis Telethon, which raises vast sums to combat muscular dystrophy. I doubt that most contributors have the foggiest idea of the extent of effectiveness of the services provided by the organization. Yet the telethon is entertaining in itself and uses both national and local personalities to elicit contributions. I once saw the work of an agency that did a fantastic job of saving the lives of impoverished babies in Bangladesh. But it went out of business because it did not develop an adequate fund-raising system. A linkage does not always exist between the satisfaction of recipient needs and the attraction of resources. The ability to perform the service and allocate available resources well does not ensure the attraction of future resources. Neither does the ability to attract resources ensure that they will be well allocated and translated into effective services.

In the profit-seeking sector, the provision of resources and the delivery of goods or services are one integrated system. A superficial comparison might be made between the sales system of a business and the fund-raising function of a not-for-profit organization. But the glaring difference is that in a business transaction, the sale is made to a recipient. In the not-for-profit activity, the "sale" is to a third party.

In this relationship, the voluntary enterprise is a middleman, or broker, linking the recipient with the contributor. The contributor donates money, time, or other resources. He or she may have a great need to give money or contribute effort to the cause. The organization pools the resources, adds value to it in some manner, and provides a service to the recipient. If the donor can donate or provide the service to the recipient, the organization has no function. But by encompassing both systems, the organization meets a unique need and justifies its existence.

There are exceptions. This model applies primarily to the service organization that exists for instrumental purposes. It does not necessarily hold true for membership clubs or trade associations, which render services in direct response to dues. But even in such cases, large amounts of labor are usually donated, and it is rare when the payment of dues is in direct proportion to the benefits received.

Aspects of the Dual Systems

In business, both donor and client are integrated in the person of the customer. The customer provides the funds and consumes the services. So profit-seeking organizations are paid for satisfying the customer. The exchange is direct, price paid for value received. Not-for-profit enterprises are agents paid by the donor to perform services for others.

I can see no particular advantage of the two-system characteristic to the ethical, conscientious manager, except perhaps in challenge and complexity. However, there are several pronounced negative aspects.

Two systems are more difficult to manage than one, just as a hook-and-ladder is more difficult to steer than a regular truck. When the ultimate consumer is not paying the bills, and the contributor is not the recipient of services, there is no built-in self-regulation. The two systems, without the integration of a single system, lack the latter's self-correcting advantage.

The two systems may not work well in tandem. Either the resource-developing system might not meet the needs of the service-providing system, or vice versa, or the two could come into direct conflict. For instance, the period of greatest need for the service might come at a time when fund-raising prospects are low. Remember, the price does not go up and down with supply and demand, because you have one market for services and another for funds. In marketing to accomodate two publics, conflicts are inevitable. Perhaps the resource-developing system determines that there would be ample donors if the services were modified to meet a more "popular" cause. An arts organization might be committed to a high-quality level of service to a limited clientele, but funds are more available for mass-audience presentations. Church members might give to a new organ fund, but the clergy could be committed to a ghetto food-bank program.

Another negative aspect of the two-system voluntary enterprise is that the two systems, each completely legitimate, may be out of balance in terms of competency or appeal. According to a 1972 study in *Time*,[57] Father Flanagan's Boys' Home was considerably better at fund-raising than at attracting clients for boy-raising—accumulating a massive surplus. It is notoriously easy to raise funds for war orphans, and difficult to get donations for long-range programs of a preventive nature. Some organizations, lean on funds but fat on pride, look down on the supply side of the organization and resent communication campaigns that lay out their needs for all to see. The resource-developing personnel might need quantifiable measures to assure donors of cost-effectiveness. The service personnel could resent the request, falling back on the traditional posture that because of their dedication they should not be called upon to account for expenditures.

An antimanagement bias persists in some quarters against controls to balance the two systems. Based on the assumption that a good cause deserves support, and therefore should not have to sell itself, it works against realistic allocations to resource development. Like the rear-wheel driver on a hook-and-ladder, the system that provides the resources has an equal opportunity to make a wrong turn and destroy the entire apparatus. But it does not have the opportunity to make many choices concerning direction. The success of the enterprise, ultimately, will be determined by how well the service-providing system does its job.

When the resource-developing side of the organization predominates, there can be a suspicion of exploitation or other wrongdoing. Indeed, with two systems and limited client control, the not-for-profit vehicle can be and has been used for fraud. Money may be given for one purpose and used for another more easily than in a business. In most business transactions the purchaser gets what he sees. In the donor/agent/client transaction, the donor and client may never encounter each other.

Incentives are different because of the two-system structure. This includes incentives for the organization itself and internal incentives available to the leadership. Contrary to popular perception, it is not the well-served, grateful clients who stimulate the contribution of resources. More often, it is a well-served, satisfied contributor who generates more contributions—both of money and of volunteer energy. Although you have to have a few appealing and appreciative clients to show, the client is not the true source of revenue, so a system primarily concerned with producing revenue has no particular need for more clients. Additional clients are problems, not opportunities, to such enterprises. They mean more work and expense. Forgotten is the fact that the success of a voluntary enterprise should be judged in terms of the services it provides, not in terms of the resources it develops.

The funds and human resources that can be tapped are, more often than not, in direct proportion to emotional appeal rather than to true utility. This aspect of the two-system structure limits the ethical manager in the internal incentives he can offer to departments, branches, and individuals. Without the direct exchange of a business transaction, no automatic tangible rewards exist; rewards must accrue in the satisfaction of performance in the providing of service.

In *Reclaiming the American Dream,* Richard C. Cornuelle[58] writes that retarded children "outnumber cerebral palsy victims ten to one, but the latter get four times as much money." *Look* magazine once observed[59] that facilities for training and supplying seeing-eye dogs provide more dogs than there are blind people who want them. It also reported, "the help given 250,000 multiple sclerosis cases was about equal to that given 11,000,000 sufferers from arthritis and rheumatism." We can't conclude that there are abuses here unless we know the kind of help supplied each group and the relative cost of each. But the figures do dramatize the two almost independent systems within these organizations. What if the same organization provided services to the two types of patients, and the same ratio of funds were developed by the fund-raising system? See the problem of appropriate allocation of resources?

An organization with an initial purpose to serve client X at location Y can be diverted from its original intention because of the two systems. The rear-wheel driver may see a fire unperceived by the driver in the cab and steer in its direction. This can be a constructive, valid evolutionary process. But if the rear-wheel driver is changing course to approach a bigger and better fire hydrant—look out! While you can't do much good in putting out a fire without a source of water, neither can you accomplish much with all the water in the world if you can't reach the fire. As Peter Drucker wrote:

> An institution which is financed by a budget—or which enjoys a monopoly which the customer cannot escape—is rewarded for what it deserves rather than for what it earns. It is paid for good intentions and for "programs". It is paid for not alienating important constituents rather than for satisfying any age group. It is misdirected by the way it is being paid into defining performance and results as what will produce the budget rather than as what will produce contribution.[60]

Management Considerations

The manager's job is to see that the systems work in tandem, meeting each other's needs, and getting to the fire in time with a sufficient water supply. This challenge is one thing that makes the voluntary enterprise manager's job very distinctive. Yet it is a characteristic setting it apart from business management, one that many do not understand. Let us detail some of the ways management must accommodate this distinctive apparatus.

First, top organizational leadership—paid and volunteer—must watch their motives and perserve their integrity. Evaluation of organizational purpose, direction, and effectiveness must be periodically structured into the planning process. If it is not scheduled and programmed, the existence of the two systems can confuse and confound the best intentions. You must have a clear, accurate, realistic statement of why the organization exists. Against this statement, your accomplishments, activities, motives, and direction must be measured. You must know what each of your systems is about, the assumptions upon which each is basing its work, and how the two are dovetailed in actual practice.

The organization, as an agent between the donor and the client, does not have the automatic evaluation mechanism of business. If a business manufactures radios and the customer buys radios and the stockholders get their dividends, the business is doing well. If a business provides furnace repairmen to camps in the Sahara and the nomads pay for their services and the investors get a good return on their money, the business is doing well. But if a not-for-profit enterprise collects cash and manufactures radios or sends furnace repairmen to the Sahara, it needs to reevaluate its effectiveness. So it must integrate an evaluation of achievements in relation to purpose into the formal management process.

In planning, the organization does not necessarily need to stick with its original purpose. But it needs to be intentional and precise in making any change in its course and to see the course reflected in its purpose as modified or restated. If the organization is off target and believes it should be, it should take conscious action to move the target to its true point of aim.

Second, recognize that you must have two marketing plans—one for each system. One strategy will deal with the eliciting of energy in the form of voluntarily contributed money, time, and other resources from the environment outside the organization. The other will be concerned with determining the needs of clients and potential clients and responding with appropriate services. One marketing task is concerned with attracting resources and the other with proper allocation of those resources to supply needed services. Two distinct transactions are involved: one with donors, the other with clients.

Voluntary enterprises have been marketing from the very beginning. But marketing scholars and practitioners have only recently "discovered" the not-for-profit sector. So they are writing books, offering seminars, and providing consulting services on marketing for this sector. Drawing upon business practice, they are applying the terminology of business enterprise to voluntary enterprise. I do not think many experienced voluntary sector managers are astounded by concepts such as market segmentation and market surveys, but much of the terminology is new, and an organization has little to lose by a closer look at what business has learned about marketing. But beware. There are two systems and two markets in the voluntary enterprise.

Third, leadership must exercise care so that the two systems do not become two organizations with inharmonious purposes. For example, the fund-raising organization seeks expensive buildings and association with affluent and socially prominent establishment types, while the service organization seeks identity and trust among the poor and disenfranchised. When such a condition develops, the organization needs no outside enemies. It will destroy itself. Harmony and congruence of goals can be handled by aligning objectives wisely in the planning function, and by staffing carefully for selection and indoctrination. Controls must be congruent and the organization norms and culture must emphasize teamwork and coordination. When this is done properly, the rank and file will barely be aware that two systems are operating. When it is done poorly, everyone will know that something is awry.

I have found this to be particularly difficult when each system works with a different social stratum. When the fund-raisers are courting multimillionaires and multinational corporations, and the service providers are working with the subculture, there is great potential for resource attraction but also great potential for staff conflict. On the other hand, when the organization is an expressive one or in the artistic or cultural field, the givers and clients may be very congruent. Here there is less of a problem of staff disharmony.

Compensation can also be a problem. On the one hand, service-side executives will tend to be stronger in education, more experienced in the field in which the organization operates, and more difficult to replace in their specialty. On the other hand, supply-side personnel can more easily show the results of their efforts in dollars. They are in a stronger bargaining position for salaries and are more accustomed and skilled in making a financial case. Like the coach of a professional football team or the promoter of rock concerts, voluntary enterprise professionals often have to learn to live with high-salaried stars who bring in the bucks.

Next, top management must recognize that each system has its own characteristics, and the two should not be managed identically. Often entirely different types of people will be effective in the different systems. Consequently, incentives and motivations will have to be different in each. The resource-attracting side can be managed more like a business than can the service-providing side, and its controls can be more precise. An expanded explanation is beyond our present scope, but a recognition of the need for management specific to each system may open the way for dramatic improvement.

Finally, the coordination of the two systems and the allocation of resources between the two must be raised to the level of a major management function. It is not enough simply to split the classical functions down the middle and have planning, organizing, direction, and controlling activities for each system. Inserted into the sequence must be the allocating and coordinating function. In my seminars on managing organizational energy, I break this function down into the following activities:

1. *Review effectiveness.* Survey the status of both systems in current needs and objectives.

2. *Ascertain cost–benefit.* In the resource-attracting system, determine how much it costs for each unit of input (cost per dollar
   raised, cost per new dollar raised, cost per volunteer recruited,
   cost per net increase on volunteer costs by one, etc.). In the
   service-providing system, determine how much it costs to provide each service unit (cost per student, per family fed, per or-
   phan adopted, per museum visitor, etc.).
3. *Analyze the situation.* Identify the needs, expectations, resources,
   opportunities, and potential of both the resource-attracting system and the service-providing system. The more these can be
   quantified, the better.
4. *Establish criteria.* Establish the basis to be used for judging how to
   allocate the organization's resources to the two systems in the
   next management cycle. (Here is the most subjective activity in
   the process. But the more the other steps are objective and quantified, the more likely the criteria are to be effective.)
5. *Proportion energy.* Select an optimum balance between the energy
   to be provided to fuel the fires of each system, within the scope
   of the organizational purpose and philosophy.
6. *Implement modifications.* Take the necessary steps to allocate the
   resources (money, fixed and variable capital, and operating
   costs) between the two systems.

The management implications for the existence of two systems are
profound. If an enterprise has not previously recognized the reality of
this characteristic, it may explain many problems, account for some
successes, or mandate major changes.

Conclusion

A voluntary enterprise lacks the integrated single system of a business. Ultimately, its success will depend upon how well its service-
providing system works. But services require adequate resources. The
resource-attracting system and the service-providing system of voluntary organizations must function equally well for the success of the
organization.

A two-system organization is complex and presents built-in problems for the not-for-profit manager. For example, it is easy for such
organizations to be off course and not know it; the two systems must
work harmoniously with each other, incentives are difficult to structure,
and it can be difficult to keep such an organization on course. The

existence of two systems makes for complexity and makes the enterprise more susceptible to mismanagement than does the more clear-cut single system of commerce and industry.

Leadership should structure regular evaluation of performances and direction compared to organization purposes. It should recognize that since it has two systems and deals with two publics, it should have a marketing plan for each, and management appropriate for each. Care must be taken to coordinate the effects of the two systems and ensure harmonious purposes and relationships among the personnel of each. And the process of coordinating and allocating the resources of the total organization to the two systems in an equitable and optimum manner must be recognized as one of the major functions of management.

7

A CONSTITUENCY

"I *belong to* Mitsubishi."

This is how a Mitsubishi worker would describe his relationship to his employer in highly productive Japan, where an employee and his company make a lifetime commitment to each other. In the United States we would say, "I work *for* Exxon" or "I *am with* American Cyanimid."

We reserve the "belonging to" for our voluntary enterprises:

"I *belong to* the Junior League."
"I *belong to* the Methodist Church."
"I *belong to* the Opera Guild."
"I *belong to* the AFL-CIO."

Or indicating possession even more:

"I *am* a Mason."
"I *am* a Teamster."
"I *am* a Scout."
"I *am* a Democrat."

Voluntary enterprises have a special kind of constituency. The organization is an instrument of its constituents. Members have a special relationship to the enterprise, distinct from the stockholder, employee, or customer relationship you find in business. There is often a loyalty on the part of the constituency, and a requirement that management be accountable to it. Often the individuals feel a concurrent sense of both "belonging" and "ownership" to a greater degree than in a business enterprise.

Voluntary not-for-profit enterprises are more responsive to their constituency than they are to their clients. In a real sense, the constituents are its customers. Clients may come and go. (There are probably more clients than can be served anyway.) Clients are a cost; constituents are an asset. Since voluntarism is its chief tool, the organizations depend on constituency and must attract and hold it to survive and prosper. Therefore, satisfying the constituency is a prime consideration in voluntary enterprises, usually affecting management decisions more profoundly than satisfying clients. (In an expressive membership organization, of course, the constituency *is* the clientele and is the total focus of the activities of the enterprise.)

In many organizations, the boundaries of the constituency are difficult to define. The boundaries may expand and contract according to the circumstances of the moment. Are registered Republicans the only constituents of that party? To what extent is an independent who votes for Republican candidates more of a constituent than a registered party member who doesn't vote at all? Is a musician or music-lover who lives in the community and regularly attends symphony performances more or less of a constituent of the symphony than a person who contributes but rarely attends? For our purposes, I consider the constituency to be the body of individuals who consider themselves as part of the enterprise or who are considered by the organization as being identified with it.

The constituency is that body of individuals that constitutes the organization. The nature of this constituency can vary greatly from one organization to another. One can be a membership organization, such as a literary society, which restricts all of its efforts to serving its members, with no design to affect individuals or the society outside the membership. At the other end of the spectrum you might find an organization that focuses virtually all its efforts on some external issue, and only incidentally picks up a constituency. An example would be one of the Ralph Nader organizations. The constituency can be the power of the organization, laying down policy and designating projects to be undertaken at will, or it may represent little more than a perfunctory assemblage put together by paid professionals for the sake of appearances. Its importance, size, and value to the organization can vary. But without some form of constituency, there is no real voluntary enterprise.

In some cases, the constituency is that original group that brought the organization into being. They saw a need or an opportunity, and established an entity to serve as their instrument in meeting the need or exploiting the opportunity. But as time passes, the constituency tends to change. Some of the original group die or move away or their interest diminishes. New leaders are attracted. Purposes might shift. A metamorphosis occurs. Power can shift from one group to another. Its size could change. As the shape of the organization is modified, the role of its constituency will change. But a group of persons will continue to have a distinctive relationship to the enterprise beyond that of a stockholder, employee, or customer.

The size and vitality of the constituency can be an indication of an organization's strength and potency. The group may have a large endowment left by an earlier generation, but without a vital constituency today, it is not likely to be effective in carrying out its purpose. It may have accumulated property of real consequence, but without a concerned and involved constituency, it is not likely to grow in the attainment of objectives. Again, the purpose of such organizations is other than profit or wealth. It must influence individuals or affect society if it is to be a successful enterprise, and this often depends on its ability to attract, hold, and apply the energies of a constituency toward the completion of tasks.

The function of an organization is to elicit, store, and effectively channel energy to reach objectives. This energy may be any resource elicited to fulfill organizational purposes. It may be in the form of money, equipment, surplus funds, talent, influence, skills, or work. Energy can be found within the bounds of the enterprise or outside in its environment. The energy is utilized in both expressive and instrumental activities. The more effectively it is applied, and the more effectively it is used, the greater the benefits the organization can provide the recipients. All of the individuals involved in contributing, changing, utilizing, and benefiting from these energy exchanges make up its constituency and are potential sources of additional energy to recharge the system.

The constituency is a source of energy because of what it does and because of what it can do. It is a ready source of volunteers, money, and other resources. It is an audience for meetings, a pool of talent, a network of contacts, and a source of supporters to promote an activity, show concern about an issue, or provide information as a resource for a project. It is a sounding board for feedback, or for amplifying an idea or a position. Its mere existence can indicate concern and support for the purposes for which the organization exists. Internally, it can provide norms to prevent the abuses of extremes within the organization. As a microcosm of the general public, the constituency provides a market sample to evaluate and test the reaction of the social environment to whatever need the organization is contemplating. If the leadership cannot bring its constituency along with it on an issue or a project, it is not likely that they will have any impact on those who have not yet cast their lot with the enterprise. The constituency feels some degree of belonging, of obligation, of loyalty to the organizational purpose, and it is a valuable resource to the institutions and other entities in the voluntary sector.

At the outset, I said that people band together when they find a need that, to be satisfied, requires the help of a group. The individual both joins and remains a member because he needs the group to reach a common objective. Whether a union because of its collective-bargaining function, or a yacht club because of its moorings, the group serves an instrumental purpose that an individual could not handle alone. Membership or affiliation with a voluntary enterprise meets other needs, apart from the instrumental. It provides enjoyable activity. Cooperative effort may be so deeply imbedded in our psyche that we simply have a need for it for its own sake.

Organizational membership provides an individual with an opportunity to participate in organizational planning and problem solving and to have an influence on decisions that affect a part of his life. Listen in at an American Legion reunion of "old army buddies," or observe hospital auxiliary members who worked together in a fund drive. The conversation will revolve around humorous, difficult, or unsuccessful problem solving. Many retired executives so hunger for the kind of participation they had in their work that they "go back to work" in voluntary enterprises to feed that hunger.

Membership is an opportunity for self-development and education. An inexperienced or uninformed individual can be assigned peripheral tasks while he learns from other members. He or she can then begin climbing the ladder toward greater responsibility for the organization's success. When an established member takes a newcomer under his wing and serves as his sponsor, the process begins.

Participation in organizational life establishes "reality." It provides consensual validation. An individual needs the group so that he will have an accepting body to bounce his views off and to test his perceptions of reality. This is easily observed when a person changes his affiliation and begins to see the world from a different point of view.

Voluntary enterprises give one a sense of security. Individuals help each other and provide a sense of control over one's environment. The organization satisfies a need to belong. As a member of the organization, a person confirms his identity, gains status, and enhances his self-esteem. Examples are street gangs of boys who do not see themselves as part of the larger society, clubs for Latin Americans recently transplanted to the United States, and various fraternal orders.

Organizational membership helps the individual solve communication problems. Face-to-face communication is part of the purpose of the organization. It is necessary to accomplish its objectives, and it presents communication as a function of manageable size to the individual. College fraternities and sororities and informal residence hall bull sessions help freshmen get information and learn the expectations of an otherwise overwhelming new society. Ostracism by "sending to coventry" (withdrawing all communication) can be devastating.

The organization perpetuates cultural values and preserves the individual's integrity. Manner of dress is an easily observed manifestation. One's organization enforces dress codes—whether the individuals be lawyers, college students, hippies, members of the jet set, or a motorcycle gang.

Organizational membership meets the need for affiliation and prevents alienation. It provides support in time of trouble and often gives the members a system of values and behavioral norms. It provides certain social satisfactions and an excellent opportunity to relate to other individuals. The role of a church congregation as a mutually supportive extended family is an example. But membership in a large organization does not guarantee immunity from alienation. Within the organization, you find many small social or task groups. For individuals in the large organization to form a small group suggests that the larger organization is not meeting personal needs of recognition, sense of accomplishment, or fulfillment. The members may not be getting the kind of support needed. Association with a group, formal or informal, imparts a sense of legitimacy with regard to our own perspectives.

Membership in an organization can reduce anxiety by being a therapeutic community. It provides an established group of peers to help a person with problems and an opportunity to express feelings without rejection. In exchange for the status, security, and other psychological benefits that the organization provides, it expects the individual to conform to its values, customs, and norms. The husband "in the doghouse" who goes to his club or has a night out with the boys is a classic example.

Organizational membership gives the individual a functional identity. Not only does the organization provide services desired by society, it also serves as a means of binding the individual into the interrelationships from which society is built. Consider how often you have based your image of an individual on the information you have concerning his organizational affiliations.

Organizational membership may be seen as serving an individual's self-interest. Voluntary enterprises are notoriously "political" in their makeup. Many are pegged at specific places in the socioeconomic strata of a community. So membership provides a stronger base and a group identity as a means of increasing chances for success at one activity or another.

Aspects of Belonging

To an organization as a whole, a constituency is an asset to the leadership of the organization. At a particular time, the existence of a constituent body can have both positive and negative aspects.

The voluntary nature of the constituency should not be overlooked. They have joined, volunteered, contributed, or benefited by their free will. Coercion or financial reward does not normally account for their affiliation. To the same degree to which they have voluntarily committed themselves, the organization is truly a voluntary enterprise. The individuals are bound together by something other than legal constraints or financial compensation.

Voluntary organizations almost always play a secondary role in the lives of the constituents—of less urgency than family or vocation. Their interest in the enterprise is usually specialized when compared with the wide range of their potential.

The constituency is, collectively, a group to which the volunteer leadership and the paid staff should be accountable. It might not be sufficiently well organized to exact accountability, and it might not be sufficiently cohesive to express itself precisely. But, over time, it is the constituency that can exercise sanctions that affect the ultimate success of the leadership. At a low level, leaders may temporarily ignore the constituency. At a medium level, leaders could manipulate the constituency to their own ends. But truly effective leaders will ultimately succeed by involving the constituency and bringing it along with them in attaining and achieving the objectives of the enterprise.

The value of the constituency as a resource for the organization can be dramatized by putting their contribution in financial terms. What would a specific project or a given week's activity have cost if there were no constituency? What if every hour of work, every bit of influence, every idea, every phone call and conversation had to be paid for at the going rate? A few minutes' contemplation will often expose the great resource of the constituency for what it is. (If such an exercise shows that your organization benefits little from the constituency, perhaps the enterprise should stir the embers and breathe life into it, so it can flame up to its potential.) Congresswoman Lindy Boggs told me that in the beginning of the Head Start program the professionals and managers were rather complacent about the significance of voluntary action. "But the minute they began to see what they could do in terms of dollar signs, they began to respect volunteer effort a great deal more, and to channel it into greater service."[61]

The constituency sets the culture and the norms of an enterprise. An organization with a constituency made up primarily of wealthy, "uptown" Republican Episcopalians can no more break its cultural pattern than can one with a blue-collar, "across the tracks," poor Democrat constituency. Be it activist, exclusive, liberal, ethnic, or regional, the dominant culture of the constituency will permeate the fabric of the enterprise and pervade the way it sets policy, selects personnel, and carries out its every activity. Working in the other direction, certain causes will attract certain types of constituencies at certain times. For example, remember the "radical chic" of the 1960s, when many of the wealthy and famous provided financial support for the Black Panthers? Could that have happened ten years later? Five years earlier? Causes and organizations may be "in" or fashionable among various cultural groups. Like any other fashion, their fortunes can ebb and flow according to the dictates of the time—or of the fashion-setters.

Obviously, the nature of the constituency and its effect on the organizational culture also influences other characteristic distinctives of voluntary not-for-profit enterprises. The very existence of a constituency makes the organization political by nature. The constituency influences the social climate of the organization, makes an impact on its purposes, adds to its complexity, and day by day affects the way the management makes decisions and carries out policy. Many organizations *are* their constituency—working to attain specific ends through the instrumentality of the structure of the enterprise.

But the constituency can be dead weight. Shackled to progressive leadership like a convict's ball and chain, it can inhibit progress or actually cause the demise of an otherwise viable enterprise. This happens when the organizational purpose and opportunity are ill-matched with the constituency. Such a condition could result from poor judgment, could be a product of evolutionary forces, or could simply be the result of the passage of time. Poor judgment might attract conservative constituents to a basically liberal cause. Evolution can lead a dormant membership downhill, while a progressive staff is moving uphill. An aging constituency with title to property might reach a point where its interests and energy level are out of harmony with the stated purposes of the enterprise. Leadership can find itself, with all the necessary ingredients for a magnificent banquet, locked into a small constituency that wants only a cup of tea.

It is common to find longtime members whose ability to make

positive contributions has passed. At this point, their keen feelings of ownership, which were previously an organizational asset, could now move over into the liability column. As my friend Murray Fincher, a retired vice-president of the telephone company, said, "They look upon the organization as 'their baby' . . . and have a tendency to dictate how it should be run." He added, "This feeling of ownership brings about a resistance to change, a discouragement to recruit new blood."[62] Whatever the status of the individual, his desire for influence on organizational direction can be either a positive or a negative factor. The emotional identity with the enterprise is a potent force, and there is no guarantee that its direction will always be aligned with that of the management.

Because an organization counts on the expressive needs of its constituency, a certain amount of its resources must be allocated to feeding those needs. As I have suggested, this is part of the purpose of the organization, and it should be recognized in a straightforward manner in any statement of objectives. But the more significant the social and expressive side of the organization, the greater the tendency to respond in the direction of that side to the disadvantage of providing a service to clients. There is only so much energy, and it is leadership's responsibility to determine the optimum allocation of that energy and to proportion its expenditure accordingly.

Management and Constituency

With this characteristic of voluntary enterprises, we are dealing with an area that simply does not exist in business. In addition to attaining objectives that have to do with the development of revenue and the provision of services, the manager is head of an organization made up of people who are not employees. He must keep them interested, involved, motivated, and even inspired. He must worry about the size of the organization, its rate of growth, and its morale. He may exceed his quantitative objectives by 100% and may produce a surplus in the treasury. But he could be out on his ear if the organization does not have faith in him or hope for the future.

Let me suggest a few specifics in regard to the manager's relationship to constituency. I will deal with his need to keep it in touch with the past, to work with it in the present, to give it a stake in the future, to build cohesion, and to help it to grow.

The constituency of an enterprise is a resource not to be wasted. If its heritage is rich, its status high, and its record illustrious, it has capital that can pay high interest. If you do not appreciate this asset, think of the difficulty of attracting leaders with clout, workers with time, and contributors with the big bucks to an organization with a blemished past. There are simply too many options. If it is a choice between the Metropolitan Opera and the Cosmopolitan Opera, the Met will prevail. If there is a choice between the Boy Scouts and the Young Guiders, the Scouts will win the toss. People like to feel they are in a tradition of great deeds and illustrious personages, and that the baton they carry has been passed on from one distinguished hand to another.

Ceremonies and rituals give individuals a tie with the past. Induction or initiation rites are important, as are rituals when an individual moves from one level to another. Though groups tend to develop these rituals automatically, wise managers have often developed rituals and ceremonies, and have even invented "traditions." For example, when the Air Force Academy was established, it began with a certain number of "traditions" copied from the pattern of West Point and Annapolis.

Even past failures, if they were heroic enough, can become assets. Look what Texas has done with the Alamo—a battle that they lost definitively, partially because they didn't send reinforcements! The past can be honored in organizational literature, in speeches, and in annual ceremonies. It can aid present leadership when it is passed on in the organizational folklore. It builds loyalty above and beyond the daily routine, ensures continuity of purpose, and provides built-in momentum.

The key word for the present is *trust*. There must be public trust of the organization. The constituency must trust the management, and members of a task group must trust each other. I am not talking about a low-level trust that money is not being stolen and lies are not being told. Rather, I refer to a trust of motives and commitment. The ties that hold the organization are rarely stocks and bonds, contracts and agreements, or dollars and cents. The ties are ties of trust, and trust is an outgrowth of integrity. Not only must there be a valid basis for trust, there must also be a perception of trust and integrity. If members feel there is a lack of sincerity in either purpose or methodology, they will fade away. This is a voluntary enterprise. No one must join, must work, or must give. Violate trust, or allow exploitation to rear its head, and they will voluntarily disappear.

If you or the organization lacks integrity, start looking for another business. You can fool some of the people all of the time, and all of the people some of the time, but no one is sufficiently talented at acting to fool all of them all of the time. Water cannot sink a ship unless it gets inside the hull. No temporary gain is worth the cost if the price is your integrity. Macaulay said that the measure of a person's real character is "what he would do if he knew he would never be found out." Individual integrity and organizational integrity builds a wholeness and a character for which there is no substitute.

The course of the organization depends on its constituency having a stake in the future. I like that analogy—stake, driven deep into the ground of the future. Tied to that stake is a sturdy cable on which you will pull, drawing yourself into that new era. Without hope, why spend energy now? Hope is instilled in the hearts and minds of the constituency by clear communications of the information and inspiration concerning what tomorrow holds for those who persevere in working for the purposes of the present. Goals must be challenging, yet attainable. You can fall short of a goal for a year or two, but hope will be deflated if time demonstrates that the goals are unrealistic and unreachable.

Hope is not limited to the organization itself. It also applies to large units of the enterprise, to small task-groups, and to individuals. Each needs that stake in the future. They must be fed today. They must have hope for more and better in the future. Every unit and every individual needs an incentive. Each should be able to see some sort of "career ladder" that can be climbed to that even better time. This is a major reason why an organization needs to expand, and why growth permeates an enterprise with interest, excitement, and vigor. For with growth there is change and an opportunity for everyone to climb that ladder as new recruits fall in behind on the lower rungs.

Cohesion is vital in dealing with the constituency. Cohesion is the force that holds the members of the constituency together. Individuals will be attracted to and remain in the organization and the organization will remain viable when the cohesive forces are stronger than the disruptive forces. The individual will be loyal to the whole as long as the body provides acceptance, security, congeniality, status, expressive satisfaction, and the achievement of meaningful instrumental goals. Human beings are naturally gregarious, and a little thoughtful encouragement on the part of management in the absence of strong disruptive forces will allow cohesive factors to operate. The ability of the leadership to communicate the significance and purpose of the organization will affect the cohesive bond. The grip that the purpose has on its constituents will vary with the changing needs of the individual and the immediacy and importance of the organizational purpose. For instance, an individual who joins an association in order to become better established in his industry will have less need for the association at a later date when he has become established. An organization founded to combat a prevalent disease will lose cohesion once the disease has been brought under control.

Members of the constituency join in order to meet certain social needs. The greater the degree to which the member builds friendships and satisfies desires for communication and affiliation, the stronger the bond. The greater the knowledge of each other's personal lives, joys, and sorrows, the stronger the glue that holds them together. While such experiences can occur automatically, opportunities can be created to encourage them. An extended amount of time together seems to have a positive effect on cohesion. The greater the time, the greater the bonding. Whether the members work together sporadically over a long period or intensely over a shorter period, the amount of shared activity is significant. Often when polls are taken of retired employees, the organization finds that it is not the work that the retirees miss, but the interaction with their colleagues. In one case a retired senior vice-president said, "Please do not send me the annual report. Send me the gossip. I miss the people I could not stand."

Meeting, eating, drinking, and having fun together builds cohesion. On the one hand, such behavior is evidence of cohesion, and on the other, such occasions for comradeship can also produce it. Church suppers, state dinners, formal toasts, the Indian peace pipe—all of these occasions facilitate friendship and establish cohesion and trust.

The magnetism of a leader contributes to cohesion. This is one reason why the charismatic style of leadership often works well in a voluntary enterprise. Such a leader epitomizes the value system of the organization, and his own value system. He serves as a role-model, an individual to be copied and emulated. The leader sets a pattern and a pace for the members, and provides a magnetic core that holds them together as a unit. A careful allocation of time and energy for the manager to fit into this role is not wasted. It builds motivation, instills loyalty, provides a degree of inspiration, and, if he associates well with individuals, it can build morale.

If individuals have pride in their organization, they will either develop their own symbols or respond well to symbols offered to them. The symbols might include insignia, uniforms, flags, rings, pins, armbands, or distinctive scarves and neckties. Such symbols provide psychological separation, which identifies them with the organization and sets them apart from others. The development of an organizational folklore, "in" jokes, and distinctive behavior and speech patterns is also evidence of cohesion or can be utilized to build it.

Growth does all sorts of good things for an organization. Growth in size of the constituency is one way for an enterprise to improve, to become more effective, and to create an interesting and exciting environment in which to work. Voluntary enterprises do not have to depend on growth exclusively or on the kind of stimulus–response relationship that a business has to its customer. When a business seeks to grow, it expends a given amount of money with the expectation that, spent effectively, it will produce more income than the cost—that is, a profit. But each time growth is attempted, there is a relatively low exchange-type ratio of stimulus to response: for instance, a ratio of 1:1.5—for each dollar spent there is a dollar and a half returned. Even in cases where the profit is considerable, the capital of the organization itself must still be expended as a stimulus. Because a voluntary enterprise has a constituency upon which it can draw for resources, utilizes volunteers to accomplish its tasks, and has a relatively unlimited access to resources, it is not limited to the same degree of stimulus–response expenditure for growth. A ratio of 1:10 is routine—in cases where one dollar spent in fund-raising will produce ten dollars in contributions. For example, dramatic ratios occur with virtually no direct costs when an endorsement, an idea, or an effective appeal by an unpaid volunteer results in income.

A voluntary enterprise is a living system. It is an organism rather than a machine. It has the ability to reproduce itself. As an open system, importing energy from its environment, it has a unique way of attracting resources.

An organization is a group of groups. Think for a moment about your own and recognize it as made up of groups of people who enjoy working together at a variety of tasks. An organization is an organism made up of cells in the form of such groups. Though these groups grow by attracting individuals, the larger organization grows by adding groups—groups that can attract, hold, and accomplish tasks with people. The cells that make up a larger organization are these task groups. Growth can be built as an integral part of an organization by planting small groups, each of which can grow to full size. If a task group is too small to do its job, a well-led group will attract enough workers. But once it has enough members to accomplish its task, and there are more individuals than can satisfactorily communicate and interact with the other members of the group, it will stop growing.

So for maximum growth, groups should be planned that are large enough to survive and survive long enough to grow, but that in the beginning are really too small for their task. Then, when they reach full strength, a new group is started with a nucleus from the old.

All relationships between management and constituency must be steeped in good two-way communications. The management must not underestimate the constituency's intelligence or overestimate its information. The constituency is almost always capable of better judgment than it is given credit for, but has less knowledge about the organization than the leadership expects. People "in the know" at the top who make a one-time announcement about a new policy, procedure, or program become so immersed in the topic that they assume the membership or other segment of the constituency is as well informed as they are. The flow of information to the constituency is subject to a great amount of interference or "noise" in the form of personal concerns, competing activities, or quantity of information. Many never hear the official pronouncement but do hear the unofficial rumors. It is almost impossible to inform them too many times about an important matter.

Listening is the other half of a communications system. In a voluntary enterprise, the leadership's responsibility to listen to the constituency may be greater than its responsibility to transmit information. If both the paid and the volunteer leadership are to be sensitive to the attitudes of the constituency, they must constantly listen to its voice. They must listen constantly, but especially to the constituency's response to messages from the top. New proposals must be run up the flagpole, and care should be taken to see who salutes how quickly and with how much enthusiasm. Good two-way communication is the medium by which individuals are able to work as an organization, and it is management's responsibility to listen as well as to speak.

Conclusion

The existence of a constituency with a special relationship to the organization is a characteristic that sets voluntary enterprises apart from business organizations. The organizations are dependent on their constituency and are usually more responsive to them than to their clients. It is a source of energy for the organization, and the organization's success often depends on the degree to which it can elicit and apply that energy toward the accomplishment of its objectives. Individuals are drawn to an organization and become part of its constituency for various reasons—some expressive, others instrumental.

There are both positive and negative aspects to having a constituency. But positive or negative, it is a factor with a strong influence on the nature of the enterprise and its ability to achieve its goals.

Since business managers do not have this special kind of constituency, voluntary enterprise managers must have skills not required of managers in business. A voluntary enterprise manager must relate the constituency to its past, and inspire it in relation to its future, as well as lead it in the present. He must build and sustain cohesion so that it holds together, and build growth into its system so that it will stay healthy and motivated.

8

MONEY MATTERS

Some psychologists maintain that people seek other rewards besides money. However, I haven't been able to get those same psychologists to expound their theories at a management conference for less than a $200 fee.

George Odiorne[63]

Odiorne missed the point. Psychologists expect a standard fee only in a situation in which someone will make a profit on their effort. But, believe me, the same psychologists have delivered much the same speeches on an "expense only" basis—or less—for not-for-profit groups.

Money is a means in a voluntary enterprise, while in a business it is an end. Reduced to essentials: A not-for-profit organization seeks to utilize a finite amount of money to provide an optimum quality of services. On the other hand, a profit-seeking enterprise produces goods or provides services to produce an optimum profit above its costs, as a return on investment. It is a matter of direction. One generates the money in order to do the job. The other does the job in order to generate the money.

For example, the Harkness Oil Company and the Coalition for Senior Adults may both seek to raise a million dollars to spend on energy. The oil company invests the money to drill into the Austin chalk formation in South Texas. They expect to recoup their money in an 18-month period and produce a two-million-dollar profit. The not-for-profit group is concerned about the rising fuel costs of the elderly. They seek the money to help their constituents pay their fuel bills. Both amounts of money pay for energy. One sought the money to provide a service. The other went through a process to produce money.

The word *profit* has a very specific meaning. Here I am not using it as a synonym for benefit or utility or end result. Rather, it is that which is left over after all the financial costs have been subtracted from all the financial receipts. Profit is the bottom line on a profit-and-loss statement. Profit is the net output of a business enterprise. As such, it can be withdrawn from the business if the owner chooses.

A not-for-profit organization, by definition, does not have profits. It provides benefits. It may have a balance when the costs are subtracted from the income. But this surplus is, by law, dedicated to providing additional services or benefits, and it is not returned to investors or to an owner. The net output of a voluntary enterprise is the service it provides. If at some time there is a financial surplus, it may not be withdrawn from the organization.

Money is a medium of exchange. Time, materials, services, knowledge, and many other things can be assigned a monetary value and then may be exchanged for dollars. An organization—be it profit-seeking or not-for-profit—uses money every day. Money is the currency for which a person trades his time or knowledge, then uses it to buy the goods or services provided by others. Money plays a vital role to a greater or lesser degree in both sectors as a medium of exchange. Both organizations need buildings, equipment, supplies, telephones, and paid workers. Both need checkbooks, financial records, bookkeepers, accountants, financial reports, and audits.

Money plays one role in the drama of business, quite another in voluntary enterprises. The difference has to do with direction, not with the financial transactions inside the organization. The overriding concern and measure of success in business is how well money produces money by providing goods or services to regenerate itself. For example, in 1975 a Louisiana man borrowed $200 from his father-in-law. He drove his pickup truck to Houston, Texas, where he purchased six 55-gallon drums of chemicals at a wholesale price. He went through the oil fields in South Texas and Louisiana selling his chemicals. With the money he received, he paid back his father-in-law, purchased six more drums of chemicals, and repeated the process. By 1980 he had built his business to $2½ million a year. The sales directly contributed to regenerating and expanding the process.

In the voluntary sector, success is measured by how well an organization provides services for its members or clients. Some types of voluntary enterprises succeed when they supply services for which the consumer is unable to pay at all. Not-for-profit organizations are "in business" to maximize service. Business and industry exist for the sake of economic performance. In voluntary enterprises such as hospitals, churches, universities, or social service agencies, economics is a restraint.

This is not to say that business is concerned only with money. The more profitable and secure the business, the more attention it gives to a hierarchy of secondary purposes, such as the welfare of employees and its responsibility to better society. Even on the economic side, short-range concerns can compete with profit. Profit sometimes must take a back seat to growth in sales or to an increased share of the market. But before attention can be given to other economic or to noneconomic matters, the firm must make a profit. That is its reason for being. It is the presence or absence of a profit that makes it a business in the first place. Attention can indeed be given to other purposes, but only after profit is secure. For example, entrepreneurs who are establishing their own business give little time or money to voluntary enterprises. Evidence shows that they exercise little social responsibility when compared to established companies with profitable track records.

In the late 1960s the Department of Labor precipitated the formation of an organization called the National Alliance of Businessmen (NAB). It was a quasi-voluntary enterprise formed to open up job opportunities in the business sector. Large and small companies were encouraged to hire disadvantaged young people for temporary summer jobs and to hire the hard-core unemployed on a long-term basis. Government funds were available to subsidize the employment, but still a minor economic burden fell to the employer. One of the first national presidents of NAB was the head of the Chrysler Corporation. His appointment was accompanied by a great deal of hype. Simultaneously, Chrysler committed itself to hire hundreds of the hard-core unemployed and to provide a training and counseling program to help them succeed on the job.

Then Chrysler encountered business difficulties. They canceled the hard-core employment program while their president was at the helm of NAB. First things had to come first. Chrysler's business was business. It was not a social agency. Thousands of other firms in the program, their profit picture in good focus, were able to meet their secondary "corporate citizenship" objective.

Voluntary enterprises have different kinds of goals from business, and money is important in reaching those goals. The enterprise seeks money too—to perform the services for which they exist. The enterprise will accomplish as much as it can with the money and will spend as little as it can to generate additional funds.

Nonprofit should not be confused with *noneconomic*. Like a business, a not-for-profit enterprise competes for resources with other organizations. The continuation or expansion of the organization may require the accumulation of capital. Any pricing they do must be in relation to similar services. Their wage and salary policy is responsive to the same factors that influence the employment market in business.

Most voluntary enterprises are given money for promises of what they will accomplish with it in the future. Efforts to get contributions for work completed and paid for (to cover a deficit) are especially difficult. Business, on the other hand, is paid for the results of its efforts. But whether the payment comes before or after performance, payment is applied to the cost of performance.

A business gets it capital from investors and creditors. The investors expect a capital gain, and creditors expect interest. Once a business begins to produce or distribute goods or provide its services, sales revenue provides funds for its operations plus a financial return for the investors and creditors. The voluntary enterprise gets revenue from donors and provides services to clients. Since the donors and clients are usually not the same, voluntary enterprises lack the integration and market test of business.

Influences of Money

The difference in the function of money has influences in not-for-profit, in contrast to profit-seeking, enterprises. Some influences are good, some are good, some are bad, and many are simply different.

Money is not discussed as much in a voluntary enterprise with a balanced budget, since something else takes the place of money as the object of all its activity. A serious money shortage is an equally pervasive topic in both organizations; in a financial boom, however, money is not spoken of as much in the voluntary sector. In the not-for-profit culture in most fields, it is not good form to discuss your personal prosperity. Perhaps this is due to the fact that ostentatious behavior can have an adverse affect on both attitudes of constituents and receipts from contributors.

This characteristic affects the pricing policy of those organizations that charge for their services. A profit-seeking endeavor must recover both its direct and indirect cost in the price charged to the customer. A not-for-profit project will charge for a variety of reasons, but it does not necessarily have to cover all costs. A teaching program may charge the students a nominal price for their books. The price may not equal their cost, but it gives the students an incentive to take care of them. A registration fee may be charged for a subsidized seminar to cover the direct costs of personnel and materials, and to ensure that those who make reservations show up. I once produced an opera written by the Metropolitan's basso, Jerome Hines. The ticket sales were projected to cover only 50% of the costs. The rest was subsidized by contributions.

Voluntary enterprises are slowly beginning to install cost-accounting systems. In cost-accounting, charges are entered for interest on invested capital and depreciation on property and equipment. Such expenses have been neglected in computing costs, so tuition at not-for-profit schools and the charges made by many other institutions bear even less relation to true costs than the public generally assumes.

Traditionally, voluntary enterprises do not pay their employees well compared to business. If an organization wants to provide a quality service, this doesn't make much sense. If the staff works with many volunteers who multiply the paid workers' efforts, they need to be especially well qualified. If the enterprise has a good and lofty purpose, then it should fairly compensate those who commit themselves to it as a full-time career. Often educational requirements are high, hours are long, and responsibility is heavy. Then why is pay often low?

One reason is that if salaries appear to be out of line on the high side, contributors may feel they are being exploited. So top management is not often paid what equal responsibility would bring in business. Employees at all levels who work shoulder to shoulder with volunteers are intermixed with individuals who get no pay at all. This acts as a depressant on salaries. Voluntary enterprises have only recently begun to stress the importance of the management function and the contribution it makes to effectiveness. They still rarely think in terms of net financial (and other) benefits that a higher-priced manager might bring to the enterprise. Compensation is not often viewed as a motivating device. There is a stigma attached to commissions, bonuses, not-for-profit versions of profit-sharing, or other financial incentives.

The appreciation given to many not-for-profit staffers for their loyalty, commitment, and dedication is often nullified if they get fat paychecks. Higher pay may be perceived as less funds available to provide services. When a business executive demands a higher salary or the workers on the line go on strike, the business can pass the increase on to their customers. A voluntary enterprise cannot. That is not what the contributors give their money for. The budget and financial statements are under public scrutiny. Every employee's compensation is in a goldfish bowl. The organization owes its constituency an open-door, no-secrets, financial picture, and it is there for all to see. Though there is a feeling that the compensation picture is improving, it is still not in the same league as business.

The role of money in business forces attention to cost-effectiveness. For example, an auto maker will not change the specifications of a part that will cost more without going through a rigorous cost–benefit analysis. In contrast, the voluntary enterprise might be negligent in its attention to cost in relation to results. Since money is not the end product, a degree of neglect can exist in the efficiency with which it is used.

Paradoxically, in a voluntary enterprise, money will gravitate not to where it will accomplish the most but to rescue the current casualty. It is often spread like a salve on a past failure and is denied to a robust success. When a project founders, the usual response is to redouble the efforts and prop it up financially. In business, by contrast, the more successful an effort, the more money it has for the next round. Perhaps the voluntary sector needs the discipline of business, which allows the unproductive, the obsolete, and the unwanted to die, so that the successful can prosper. It gets back to giving money for intentions and promise of effort rather than for results. There is no good management reason for this, and it is a trap to be avoided.

Another difference is in the way the two types of enterprises get their capital. A voluntary enterprise has no tangible way of compensating investors for their risk. (They can issue bonds or borrow money. They may do so without collateral, and with the investor's full knowledge that the money may not be repaid. But this is only a variation on fund-raising. The investor enters the arrangement in order to help the organization rather than as a means of participating significantly in any gain.)

A business, on the other hand, may attract risk capital provided by parties who anticipate a return in equity or interest far greater than could be expected in a conservative investment. For instance, a few years ago companies in the bioengineering field went public and their stock skyrocketed. Stock in companies with book values at $5 a share sold at $40 and $50.

In the not-for-profit sector, risk capital may come in the form of a grant from a foundation, the government, or a wealthy individual. It can be given on a restricted basis for the construction of a building, for example. The donor does not expect a return. But in constructing a building, or paying for certain specific programs, the donors participate in the objectives of the recipient. Looking at it another way, a not-for-profit foundation is utilizing the recipient as an agent in achieving its own ends. As Richard Cornuelle wrote:

> Foundations think of themselves as America's laboratory. They pay for risky research; they experiment; they promote new things and challenge the status quo. Their strength is their flexibility. They can't seek profit; they don't have to seek public acclaim. They can try damn-fool things. Created by profit from the commercial sector, they provide the distinctive risk-capital of the independent sector.[64]

Large corporations may give grants for research or for education in certain fields with the expectation of a potential indirect return. For instance, energy companies contribute large sums to geology and petroleum engineering departments of universities. General Electric, IBM, and Texas Instruments contribute heavily to computer science programs. Though there is no direct financial return, as in an investment, the corporation might benefit by the improved flow of knowledge or personnel in their field of interest.

Since large grants normally go only to well-established institutions and organizations, the new not-for-profit enterprise often gets its "venture capital" in another form. A person with a dream works without pay, using his own resources to sustain himself. Like the entrepreneur starting his own business, he takes a great personal risk. But unlike the business entrepreneur, he does not find that success brings wealth. For his risk and commitment he is often repaid in love, honor, and esteem. In other cases, the organization outgrows him. The entrepreneurial skills that allowed the organization to get under way must be replaced with management skills that he may not possess. If he is not willing to relinquish management, a power struggle ensues. If he loses, there is heartbreak for him, and trauma and scars for the organization. If he wins, the organization may fail or cease its growth. For example, the Ford Motor Company outgrew Henry Ford, and he could not cope with what was happening to the company and the industry. As late as 1948 Ford Motor Company was operated as a personal company. The company bank account was Henry Ford's bank account. It was going downhill until the successful transition to Henry Ford II enabled the company to function with an effective management style.

Implications for Management

Obviously, the same money decisions do not apply in an organization that seeks to maximize money as in one that seeks to maximize service.

I once served on mayor's committee dealing with problems of the school system. Students were not learning as they should. Citizens were unwilling to be taxed for improvements. We reviewed a study conducted and paid for by the business community. It cost a great deal and was a commendable effort at community service.

But the study restricted itself to finances and tangible assets, the kind of things that accountants know best. Every one of the group's recommendations could have been carried out without directly affecting the quality of the subject—the student. The study design failed to consider sufficiently that the proper output of the school system was not an improved financial statement but improved minds. This is not to say that the recommendations were not constructive. I just wish that some of their management skills could have been applied to the management of the system's human resources.

Intermixed within a not-for-profit enterprise are successful individuals attuned to the management of profit-seeking enterprises. The more confident and successful they are at what they know best, the more likely they are to influence the organization's direction. It can be difficult for them to shift gears and be comfortable in an environment in which financial statements are relegated to a secondary status. Their expertise can indeed be useful to the voluntary enterprise. But if they do not take the time to appreciate some of the differences in managing the two types of organizations, there will be problems. They can lead the group into error or drop out in frustration. The dropout might not always be complete. It is often a retreat in which the skilled manager, who could make a profound contribution, offers a few suggestions about investments or acts as a watchdog over potential waste.

So, in the planning function, the purposes must be clearly stated. There should be no doubt as to what constitutes organizational success. Financial and other resources should be shown as means to ends, and the ends described as specifically as possible. In defining objectives, selecting strategy, and setting policy, there should be no doubt as to the ultimate purpose of the activities.

The service could be provided but the hoped-for result not attained. The student could refuse to learn, the old person might not become happy, the population could ignore the safety advice, the patient might die, or the youth could commit another crime. But those involved in planning and evaluation must remember that a failure to achieve desired results is a problem endemic to the voluntary sector. If the group's outputs were predictable in terms of value, their function might be performed at a profit. Without the not-for-profit purpose, the attempt might not be made at all. At the outset of planning, it must be clearly understood that success or failure can't be determined in financial terms alone.

This fact must be imprinted on the minds of board members, managers, and volunteer leaders—the decision-makers of the organization. It must be considered in the design of the financial accounting system, and there should be a system of "accounting" for both nonfinancial resources and nonfinancial outputs.

The distinctive place of money has an impact on the various personnel categories. Since board members do not normally benefit financially, those who agree to serve do so out of other motives. Unless they hope to write the insurance or supply the cafeteria, they serve for satisfaction, for service, for reputation, or simply because they enjoy it.

Paid management knows it will never get into the financial big leagues of stock options or other equity participation, even if they are responsible for doubling the income every year. It stands to reason that if the top management's every thought is not attuned to profit maximization, they cannot be as concerned with cost-effectiveness as their business counterparts.

Often the professional staff will tend to take finances for granted. Their efforts will be expended in the interest of quality and the satisfactions of the work itself. They tend to look at the "business side" of the organization as somewhat gross, to be attended to by lesser mortals. In the language of industry and the military, the professional and technical people are "line" while in business they would be "staff."

Contributors and volunteers would not even exist if the purpose of the enterprise were to produce money. Inefficiencies cut into group services instead of into dividends. So everyone is affected by the way money is perceived in a voluntary enterprise.

It is my observation that the money side of these organizations is often neglected. Those on the service side make a line projection of their needs and desires. Goals are set, a cost is calculated, and financial resources are sought to pay the bills; occasionally, someone will be caught up in a vision of expansion and will inspire the constituency to renewed vigor. A capital-funds campaign is launched, and the organization will move upward a few notches on the ladder. Such an effort might coincide with the coming of a new chief executive. But in my experience the motivation has always been one of expanded scope or enlarged service, with the seeking of financial resources to follow. I cannot remember a call to the troops on the basis of accumulating resources—with decisions to follow as to how it will be spent. Perhaps service-first is the only sequence in which it can be successfully done.

Then there are foundations and endowments that employ high-powered resource developers, marshall the volunteer corps to amass the resources, invest them at a good interest rate, and then consider proposals for expenditures in line with the purpose. But must financial thinking always lag six paces to the rear? The wisest decision a not-for-profit organization might make could be to shift its priorities and "beef up" its capability to do this tough job well.

At any rate, the function of coordinating the allocation of resources between the service-providing and the resource-developing systems

must be raised to a high level. When I define the basic voluntary enterprise management functions, I list it right alongside planning, organizing, staffing, guiding, and controlling. Rather than merely proposing a
budget for service-side programming, then deciding what might have to
be spent in order to raise that amount, a different approach should be
taken. The approach consists of coming up with a unit-cost figure for
providing services on the one hand and a unit-cost figure for raising
money on the other. Then, in light of long-range strategies, resources
should be deliberately allocated to each of the two systems. Decisions
are made on the basis of attainment of long-term goals, rather than
immediate needs and wants of the service-providing systems.

In the directing or guiding function, money is conspicuous by its
relative absence as a motivation. I say relative because it is a motivator to
the degree to which it expresses appreciation and symbolizes status. But
in most cases, the esteem and recognition provide the motive force
rather than the cold cash itself. As evidence, consider the prevalence of
the large contributions that employees give to their own organizations.

In the control function, results must be evaluated by indicators
other than money. On the service-providing side, the entire feedback
system must be based on a currency other than dollars and cents.

Conclusion

Money is merely a means in a voluntary enterprise, while in business it is an end. A voluntary enterprise needs financial resources in
order to provide its services, but its success or failure is not based upon
its financial bottom line. An organization can have a generous increase
in revenue over expenses every quarter, yet fail miserably in attaining its
goals.

This relegates money to a secondary place. It might not always be
given the attention it deserves. This can cause problems in cost-effectiveness, in efficient use of resources, and in fund-raising. Though money affects all classes of personnel in a nonprofit organization, it lacks the
incentive-and-response power it has in business.

Management must give special attention to coordinating the
amount of funds allocated to the two internal systems in order to
achieve long-term effectiveness. In a voluntary enterprise, money plays
a vital role, but a different one than it plays in business. It is an essential
supporting actor, but not the superstar.

9

SPECIAL LEGAL STATUS

"Death and taxes are inevitable," said Halliburton.
"One out of two ain't bad," said the beggar.

Voluntary enterprises enjoy a special legal status. This may be their most taken-for-granted characteristic. Except for informal organizations and small short-term enterprises, most voluntary enterprises are constituted as nonprofit corporations. Since they provide a public service and money is only a means to them and not an end, the government grants them a status that sets them apart from enterprises that seek profits. They enjoy advantages such as freedom from taxation. Contributions to many of them are tax-deductible. In many cases, such organizations are not subject to as many regulatory restrictions as profit-seeking firms. So they are relieved of some of the burdens under which commerce and industry must labor. A businessman will quickly agree that this is an advantage that the not-for-profit executive might not fully appreciate.

Two categories of exempt organizations exist under the law: (1) private foundations and (2) other nonprofit organizations. Tracy Connors explains:

> Private foundations are subject to a number of restrictions on their activities and are subject to certain taxes, including a tax on the failure to distribute their income at a specified level. Normally, individual donors can deduct contributions of more than 20 percent of their adjusted gross income to a private foundation (unless the private foundation makes qualifying distributions within two and a half months of the end of its fiscal year).[65]

Public-supported organizations (other than private foundations), on the other hand, receive broad public support and are subject to a minimum of federal regulation. These organizations have no specific rules on the amount of surplus they can accumulate so long as it "does not become excessive."

These organizations must not be for the purpose of profit. They may be exempt from income tax if they are organized for religious, scientific, educational, charitable, or certain other purposes. No part of their net earnings can benefit private shareholders or individuals. Some of the enterprises, such as churches, church-related organizations, and those with annual receipts of less than $10,000, do not even need to be registered. Though foundations have been subject to increasing limitations, other nonprofit organizations have a relatively small amount of regulation.

Freedom from regulation goes back a long way. The church (certainly among our oldest forms of voluntary enterprise) has fought for separation from the State in many cultures. The U.S. Constitution guarantees such separation in our own country. In ancient Greece, associations were not considered entities in and of themselves. Members bore legal responsibility individually. Under this condition, there was no regulation. At a later date, there was complete freedom in Greece in the establishment of societies. Solonic law affirmed this freedom but reminded the organizations that they must be within the framework of the law.

While we think of freedom from regulation as part of the Western tradition, there have been exceptions. A political regime becomes totalitarian when it impinges on the rights of voluntary groups of individuals. Often the first sign of totalitarian motives is an attempt to suppress the right of some voluntary enterprise to express dissent or to assemble its constituency. When such moves are successful, suppression of individual citizens often follows. (This implies a lot about the role of the voluntary sector in a democratic society.)

Aspects of the Special Legal Status

The special legal status of nonprofit organizations is an asset with almost no concomitant liabilities. Nonprofit organizations simply are allowed to play by different rules.

One advantage of their special status is their freedom from corporate income tax. This allows them to retain money that a business would pay to the government unless it is derived from activities not connected to their public purpose, that is, unrelated business income. It permits them to build an endowment fund, to offer more services, or to reduce prices.

In addition to the historical tradition, nonprofit groups are able to maintain freedom from most government regulation and are free from taxation for several reasons. Many organizations provide social services in lieu of that which the government might otherwise be expected to provide. Even the expressive organizations provide a societal good, and since (theoretically, at least) the organization has no owners, taxation would be a self-defeating activity of the society.

Dean Kelley, an author and a member of the staff of the National Council of Churches, believes there is a common misconception the public has about tax exemption. In a television interview he told me, "People often have the sense that the nonprofits . . . are not carrying their fair share of the tax burden. They misunderstand the way the tax system operates."[66] He went on to explain: "Most Western societies base their revenue system on spreading the burden across the profit-producing aspects of the economy. Nonprofit groups are not part of that system. They are not sources of revenue. It isn't that they are exempted from it. It is just that they are not part of it to begin with." As a matter of reality, most organizations plow back any surplus into their operations and would have no profit to tax even if they were required to file. On this same subject Kelley also observed, "Tax exemption is not subsidization. It is simply the state's refraining from taking part of the voluntary contributions the group receives." The churches, under the First Amendment, have additional tax protection. They are not required to file tax informational returns, and they cannot be examined by the IRS except under narrow conditions that must be approved by the regional director. On the negative side, the same amendment that mandates separation of church and state also disqualifies churches and church-related organizations from many direct grants and contracts with governmental bodies.

If the organization's services are in competition with business, or if it owns a business, the advantage is dramatically obvious. For example, Loyola University of the South in New Orleans owns radio and television station WWL. Its proceeds are the main endowment of the school and provide scholarships for many of its students. Its freedom from taxation gives WWL a competitive edge that could account for its being the top television station in its market.

Some not-for-profit organizations, on the surface, appear to be businesses in the manner of their operation and the nature of their products or services—for instance, the National Geographic Society, the American Automobile Association, and many religious publishing houses.

The tax code provides that if the nonprofit organization makes a profit from a business unrelated to its exempt purpose, the income is taxable. At one time, churches were exempt from that provision, but in 1969 the U.S. Catholic Conference and the National Council of Churches asked Congress to eliminate that exemption.

A *Reader's Digest* article[67] gives other examples of not-for-profit competition with business. It cites "the many colleges and universities around the country that own motels, or lease facilities to restaurants, or stores that sell refrigerators, motorcycles and other items unrelated to education. Not only do these establishments sometimes take business away from local merchants, but the revenues are often tax-exempt." The same applies to the more than 140,000 nonprofit fraternal organizations that also operate insurance and health programs and other services that are tax-free, as long as sales are directed exclusively to members of the groups. The Knights of Columbus life insurance program, for example, has about $4 billion worth of business and the Lutheran Brotherhood about $7.7 billion.

A second and perhaps greater advantage is that gifts to public charities are tax-deductible to the giver. This is an encouragement and an incentive to any contributor. It makes it possible for an individual in the highest tax bracket to substantially assist a cause dear to his heart with a cost to himself of only 50 cents on the dollar. To wealthy persons who see the voluntary sector as a better channel than government to provide certain services, the tax break makes contributions a viable alternative to taxes. When this factor is linked to a person's desire for recognition, an institution can make a strong argument for a major gift (such as a building) to be named for the donor. Dean Kelley points out:

> The theory is that money not spent for the giver's own personal advantage is treated in the tax code as if it is not income to him. For instance, if he makes $50,000 and gives nothing, he pays the same income tax as someone who makes $55,000 and gives $5,000 of it to charity. The $5,000 he gave does not directly advantage him.[68]

Kelley gives another example:

> If someone contributes $1,000 to his or her church, and also sends a child to a school maintained by the church, that person cannot deduct the proportion of the total gift that would be equivalent to the cost of the education. That is like tuition, from which he derives direct benefit.

The special status also makes exempt organizations eligible for other benefits from the government, such as reduced postal fees and the right of some organizations to issue tax-exempt bonds. An estimated $600 million dollars annually subsidizes the lower postal rates provided to the not-for-profit organizations. Cheaper rates, usually taken for granted, allow many organizations to inform their constituencies and raise funds by mail that would be prohibitively expensive if they had to pay full price. Under certain conditions, organizations, such as not-for-profit hospitals, can raise capital through tax-exempt bonds. Individuals in the higher tax brackets can get a higher after-tax return of a lower-

interest-rate tax-free bond than on a higher-interest-rate taxable investment. Again, this is an opportunity for a wealthy individual to do well
while doing good.

Local governments exempt nonprofit groups from property taxes
and often give them reduced utility rates.

Another advantage is the absence of much onerous government
regulation and red tape. You have only to lunch with businessmen or
read business publications to learn how expensive, complicated, and
bothersome government regulations can be. Regardless of whether or not
it is necessary or good, government involvement is an expense that can
make the difference between profit and loss to a business. Edward James,
a management consultant, told me that $40 billion is spent annually in
paper work responding to U.S. federal regulations and requirements.

Though voluntary enterprises are still not subject to as much regulation as businesses, the amount of regulation is increasing. All tax-exempt organizations except churches, for example, must now file annual
informational returns—Form 990.

Of course, their not-for-profit status puts them under an obligation
to work diligently toward the purposes for which they receive contributions, and not to abuse special privileges. Other than that (which is true
of any organization), I see no negative aspects to their special legal
status.

Management Implications

Most of the implications of the special legal status of voluntary
enterprises are self-evident. A voluntary enterprise likely to be large
enough and permanent enough surely will incorporate as a nonprofit
corporation so that contributions to it will be tax-deductible. It will want
to utilize any advantageous benefits that it is due.

To incorporate as a nonprofit organization, the group should retain
an attorney experienced in nonprofit law, since the requirements and
procedures vary from state to state. The group will draw up a constitution and bylaws, and the attorney will file the proper forms with the
state. The cost of incorporation will range from $50 to as much as $400.
Often an attorney can be found who will waive his fee. These initial legal
steps will lay out the boundaries, limitations, and authorities of the
enterprise, so they must be drafted with care, with competent legal
counsel, and adopted with ample opportunity for careful consideration.

Tax-exempt status does not come automatically with incorporation.

The group must apply to the Internal Revenue Service.[69] Eligibility is contingent upon the organization's purpose and the nature of its activities. Some classes of organizations, as I mentioned earlier, have a dual advantage: Not only is the enterprise tax-exempt, but also the contributions of donors are tax-deductible. State laws generally follow the federal pattern, and in some states the organization may not be subject to sales or other taxes either.

Not quite so obvious is the need to protect the privileges nonprofit corporations currently enjoy, and to work toward increasing those advantages when it can do so within an ethical framework. For example, modifications in the tax law are proposed at virtually every session of Congress. Organizational leadership should be alert to legislation at all levels of government, and should respond accordingly. For example, as this book goes to press, various "flat-rate" taxes to replace the graduated income tax are being proposed. Many proposals would eliminate tax deductions for contributions to not-for-profit organizations. Tax deductions have an impact on contributions, and they lower the cost of giving, so voluntary enterprises should express their concern.

The special legal status must also be protected by avoiding its abuse. If the public perceives that the laws are unjust and provide unwarranted privileges, the laws could be modified to the disadvantage of the voluntary sector. For example, consider the competition of not-for-profit organizations with businesses in the same marketplace. If business leaders consistently face losses in competing with enterprises that do not pay taxes, they will fight that competition as unfair. They will seek relief in the courts or in the legislature. If that fails, they could weaken their not-for-profit competition's ability to attract contributions and community support.

The individual taxpayer also rebels when he sees tax dodgers using the nonprofit label to take unfair advantage. When an individual is caught trying to deduct the cost of educating his children by some tax dodge, or establishing a foundation for a less-than-honorable purpose, both the individual and the institution are subject to sanctions. The more often it happens, the more threatened is the sector as a whole.

Again, I am indebted to Dean Kelley, who reminded me of a new development that the Internal Revenue Service calls "Mail Order Ministries."[70] To take advantage of the tax law, groups claim to be churches. An individual gets a bogus certificate, and as Kelley says, "They deduct large contributions to the church, which in turn supplies them with food, clothing, and shelter." The government does not put itself in the position of defining what is or is not a religious purpose or activity. But the Internal Revenue Service, according to Kelley, cracks down on them on the basis that the actual use of the money goes back to the members, "and is thus operating for a private rather than a public purpose."

The special legal status is an official recognition of public trust and appreciation of the purposes of voluntary enterprises. This puts a burden on management's shoulders. The burden is responsibility for integrity in intent, honesty in communication, and high ethical practice in administering the organization. Our predecessors have passed to us the baton of a heritage that has earned respect. As we run our lap, we have the opportunity to make gains that give to our successors a better heritage than our own.

But the very high regard in which the voluntary sector is held makes it an attractive cloak for charlatans. The protective law, the lack of regulation, and the tax advantages make nonprofit organizations a tempting umbrella for those who would exploit the trust for their own advantage. Ethical managers should conduct their organizations to avoid any hint of abuse, and should join and support efforts to "police" the sector, close legal loopholes, and eliminate shady practices. Harvey Katz[71] cites many examples of corrupt individuals and ill-managed organizations that could well lead the public to become cynical about voluntary enterprises.

Conclusion

Organizational leadership often fails to fully appreciate or adequately take advantage of the fact that not-for-profit enterprises enjoy a special legal status. They are allowed to play be different rules than those imposed on business and industry.

This gives organizations in this sector significant advantages, with virtually no disadvantages. They are free from many regulations. They are eligible for lower postal rates. They are not subject to corporate income tax. But, most important of all, gifts to many of them are tax-deductible to the contributor—an incentive to both individual and corporate givers.

Management should be aware of the legal advantages their organizations enjoy, and be vigilant to protect and maximize their privileges.

10

PROFIT AND LOSS

Drop many profit-sector managers into a typical voluntary enterprise and they will react much as they would in a deep forest without a compass. Take away their "bottom line" and they go into culture shock. Without profit and loss, they have no reference point, and, like the compassless wanderer, they have difficulty in finding their direction. *Voluntary enterprises do not have profit and loss with which to monitor operational effectiveness.*

A business or industrial organization can evaluate its effectiveness as an entity by its profit-and-loss (P&L) statement. In business, most variables can be assigned a numerical value directly related to P&L. The ability to interpret most of its operations in P&L terms becomes a tool that can be used in many organizational nooks and crannies. It is a universally integrating function in business management, measuring effectiveness and efficiency. Business can evaluate most of its component operational departments or branches by the degree to which they contribute to overall profitability.

A voluntary enterprise lacks this valuable tool. The generation of profit is not the purpose of the voluntary enterprise. Profit is not its primary objective, a measure of success, or a means for choosing among alternative activities.

The use of P&L as an instrument in business is distinct from the purpose of business. Management can use P&L figures as a tool for planning, directing, controlling, and evaluating business performance.

In not-for-profit organizations, voluntarily contributed resources are elicited without an equivalent value of service provided in turn. The organization is outside of the market economy of business. So such organizations lack the pervasive presence of money as a measure of individual and unit contribution to organizational performance.

Of course, the effectiveness of any organization can be determined by the degree to which inputs produce certain outputs. But voluntary enterprises, with multiple service purposes and the difficulty in determining the market value of services, lack the unifying measurement of effectiveness. It is a serious deficiency, and one that dismays the typical skilled profit sector manager.

The typical voluntary enterprise manager, on the other hand, cannot understand what he is missing. Like the Eskimo who somehow finds his way across the trackless snowscape, he goes about his business unaware of maps and road signs. Unless and until he has experienced the precision and certainty of the one, he cannot fully appreciate the difficulty of the other.

How P&L Works for Business

In business, the effectiveness of the entire organization can be evaluated by the income it derives from its efforts. Efforts can be broken down according to their contribution to income, and income broken down and distributed according to the contribution of each responsible unit. Criteria for P&L can be established, and performance measured against them. A company can estimate the amount of resources required to produce an anticipated profit and can measure the effectiveness and efficiency of all of the units involved. P&L provides a control structure for measuring the part each unit contributes to the final product or service. As Etzioni wrote:

> Production is a rational activity, which requires systematic division of labor, power, and communication, as well as a high level of coordination. It therefore requires also a highly systematic and precise control of performance. This can be attained only when sanctions and rewards can be readily measured and allocated in close relation to performance. Remunerative sanctions and rewards are the only ones that can be so applied, because many differentials are far more precisely measurable than force, prestige, or any other power differentials.[72]

P&L has an integrating effect on the management of the organization. When different departments produce different products or services, or when they make their contribution in sequence toward a single result, profit targets can be allocated to each unit. P&L allows for the coordination of resources to complementary functions.

White, Levine, and Vlasak give an excellent example. They say that the problems of allocating resources in order to coordinate complementary functions are solved by price.

> If we consider the production of a single complex product, such as an automobile or an airplane, we see that the efforts of autonomous organizations are brought together by mechanisms that encourage "necessary" goods and services and discourage the "unnecessary." Purchasing and subcontracting are two such integrative mechanisms. Integration of the system is achieved through the linkage of specific dyads of organization in terms of reciprocal needs and demands. Even though the system is pluralistic, reasonable integration is achieved.[73]

Profit is feedback, not only in the form of data but also in the form of cash. It provides self-regulation of the business process by its own results. When everything works right, the customer provides the money to reward all who contributed, and sets up the next cycle. When the customer's needs are incorrectly assessed or improperly met, he doesn't provide that reward. Loss feeds back its message. If that message is read accurately, corrections can be made, and the product, service, or price becomes acceptable. Subsequently, positive feedback in the form of profits demonstrates the effectiveness of corrective measures.

This management tool exists in business because part of the very thing for which it exists is used to pay for the efforts required to achieve it.

In providing the services of a voluntary enterprise, the same thing simply does not exist. Only in the fund-raising system or in "profitized" functions can the control structure approximate that of P&L in business.

Advantages and Disadvantages

Consider the few advantages and then more disadvantages of the lack of P&L measuring criteria for the not-for-profit organization. On the positive side, there is the emphasis on human values apart from contribution to profit or loss. A business can, in its tireless machinelike quest for efficiency, starve the humanistic hunger in an organization. One has to look no further than assembly lines such as the Vega line at Lordstown. There, continual striving for more production has produced a cost on the human side: low morale, absenteeism, and mental fatigue. Perhaps the lack of a P&L measure makes it possible for voluntary enterprises to have their expressive side and perform their expressive functions. In general, they are more responsive to personnel management pressures than to marketing and productivity pressures. This avoids the abuses of the pressure-cooker environment where profit criteria are enforced to the extreme.

The impressive productivity of Japanese industry has attracted American business like hungry bears to wild honey. Americans examine and question and probe, looking for a secret key that they can bring back to the home shore to bolster their own lagging productivity. It is interesting that William Ouchi,[74] in a study of Japanese industry, identifies certain characteristics that are more typical of our Western voluntary enterprises than of our industry. Since many not-for-profit organizations have persisted for centuries, there are obviously some compensating values to their lack of P&L as a means of reaching objectives.

Individuals who do not work well under intense short-term accountability may find a place to be productive in the not-for-profit climate. While lack of the P&L measure is a liability for the organization, it can be an asset for certain individuals within the organizational systems. I refer not to the indolent ne'er-do-well who rationalizes poor performance but to the capable craftsman who needs a lot of time and nurturing in order to bear fruit.

Though the end sought is not economic, and resources cannot be allocated or results measured in economic terms, ends can still be attained without reference to an economic framework. The lack of a concern for the enterprise to do anything more than break even financially allows personnel to be sensitive to other values. In a voluntary enterprise, the noneconomic accomplishments are its outputs. In business, they are part of its input.

More of the negative aspects of this characteristic cluster around the concept of feedback. P&L is a common denominator and provides feedback in the profit-seeking organization, and it is lacking in the voluntary not-for-profit one. Not-for-profit management finds it difficult to control the flow of work and to improve cost-effectiveness. Without P&L feedback, it is difficult to compare across organizations, between internal systems, across departments, and from one employee to another. It results in weak internal competition for resources, and components of the organization have difficulty in relating what they do to the overall output.

Look at cost-effectiveness as an example. In business, the contribution an activity makes to profit is its yardstick of effectiveness. It is tangible. It is measurable. Its relationship to the whole may be determined on a tangible quantifiable financial basis. Therefore, when its costs in relation to its effect on the output goes beyond the tolerances set, it is easy to see where costs must be cut.

Some 15 years ago, F. W. Woolworth Co. decided to enter the mass merchandizing business and opened its Woolco outlets. But these stores were not profitable, so the company decided to close the Woolco stores.

The P&L measure showed that Woolco was not contributing to the business. After the stores closed, Woolworth again returned to profitability.

Without P&L, the not-for-profit manager has difficulty controlling costs in terms of its relation to the service provided. Closely linked to this factor is the lack of the profit incentive to employees. While profitability is not a perfect measure, it is a far more effective one than has yet been developed in the voluntary sector. It is a means for allocating resources on the basis of the contribution to results made by individuals. This is an automatic control, linking decisions and efforts to results, giving the individuals an incentive both for production and for cost control.

With P&L, comparison is possible because the same measurement is used by all of the concerned, whether these units be Jane Newhouse as compared to John Stonewall, the Avondale Plant compared to the Whitewater Shop, or General Motors compared to General Telephone. When all are being compared in measurable financial terms of profit or loss, efficiency and effectiveness are laid out for all to see and understand. Whether two employees, two internal departments, or two corporations are being compared, you are dealing, in each case, not with apples and potatoes but with dollars and cents.

Then there is competition. Several otherwise knowledgeable writers speak of the absence of competition in the voluntary sector. These statements baffle and bewilder me. If they are not competitive, then neither are piranhas, hyenas, or vultures. Voluntary enterprises compete fiercely for contributions, for volunteers, for "turf," for credit for what they do, for personnel, and for clients. (It is true that they rarely compete in the area of mass media advertising for clients. Perhaps this has misled some outside observers.) Cooperation exists among organizations with competing services. But when organizations must vie with each other for the same resources or clients, the competition can be both energetic and vicious. Consider the competition between the Sierra Club and the National Rifle Association, between the KKK and the NAACP, between the Moral Majority and the National Council of Churches, between the Democrats and the Republicans, and between adjacent colleges.

Perhaps the misconception that nonprofits are not competitive has to do with the pricing of their services. There is not the same competition in pricing that you find in business. The demand is usually so much greater than the supply that there is plenty of "business" for all. On the other hand, in cases in which the client is charged, the price is usually only a portion of the total cost. The price is often based on what the client can afford to pay, not upon what the service costs. Since the price is not expected to cover the cost, the organization is not under a strong market pressure.

External competition with other organizations is strong. However, internal competition for resources lacks an objective basis for measurement. Without the profit target and P&L measures of contribution to profit, competition among units is often highly subjective. There may be rivalry and jealousy, but there is little solid opportunity for the vibrant evolutionary forces you find in business.

Internal resources competition in business is based on the contribution to overall profitability of various products and services, different geographical branches and outlets, and various divisions and departments. At least, this is how it is supposed to work. Admittedly, in the real world of personalities, power plays, and politics, other factors affect outcomes. But theoretically, from year to year, the more profitable goods, services, or units are usually given more resources with which to expand and produce more profits. Generally, as the less profitable ones continue to be less profitable, their resources diminish. Those that produce are fed; those that do not are starved. Sometimes it is also true that this condition would produce a thorough evaluation of the unit to determine the cause and to correct it, possibly with a change in management, repositioning of the product, infusion of funds, or all of the above. This internal competition makes it possible for a business to evolve into a more viable and profitable concern. The evaluating process is possible because of internal competition for resources, based upon the contribution each unit makes to P&L. It is an honest, automatic, realistic, and somewhat ruthless system. Since the desired outcome is profit, and the undesirable outcome is loss, the P&L statement continuously provides feedback that guides the enterprise toward prosperity. It does not put much stock in how big an office is, how well educated the staff is, how pretty one is, how well people speak of the service, or whether luck was good or bad. Subjective evaluations are supposed to be given a low weight, and profitability or the lack of it calls the shots.

Voluntary enterprises then, with their lack of P&L as a tool with which to monitor operational effectiveness, do not have the automatic evaluating process of internal competition for resources. Dale D. McConkey[75] says: "It's a management truism that an organization is sick when it fails to establish competition for resources or has more resources than it knows how to utilize. Unlimited resources represent a contradiction to good management."

Without internal competition for resources among its various components or departments, internal competition is weak and ineffective in providing guidance. If the purpose of an institution is to educate youth, and not to make money, politics and personalities will influence a dean more than an objective comparison of the contribution of the history department against the English department. If its purpose is to heal the sick, how does the hospital administrator measure the X-ray department against the emergency room? If the purpose is to preserve our heritage, how does a museum manager compare the Egyptian collection with the Impressionist wing?

Another negative aspect of the lack of P&L has to do with personnel—both staff and volunteers. They have difficulty, in organizations lacking quantifiable objectives, relating what they do to the organizational output. They have a corresponding difficulty in choosing among alternatives. What criteria do they use? What do they emphasize? This often results in confusion between reality and perception, between activity and accomplishments, and between low payoff and high payoff effects. Personnel in voluntary enterprises often feel that it does not matter so much what they are busy about as long as they are busy about something. They often "cop out" by making the false assumption that if they produce less, what they produce will be of higher quality. They find it difficult to relate the results of their activity to the measurable output of the entire organization. With the profit motive and the use of the P&L contribution, employees in a business can relate what they do to an output figure. For example, Delco Radio changed from an assembly line to a job enrichment method, which allowed employees to assemble an entire radio. The employee knew which radio went into which kind of car and how much it cost. Their behavior, their activities, and their performance were then oriented to and aligned with the organizational purpose. In many voluntary enterprises, the only automatic orientation and alignment has to do with attitude. And attitude does not automatically result in optimum performance.

Market pressure, reflected internally in the business sector by the P&L, theoretically serves a unifying and integrating purpose on a day-by-day basis. This should reduce the level of bickering and feuding. Ideally, it applies a constant pressure on the units and individuals within the organization to help keep costs down and push productivity up. As feedback on how well they are doing in relation to the market, the right behaviors can be rewarded and the wrong ones disciplined. In voluntary enterprises this opportunity is usually lacking, unless it is in a fight for survival against an outside competitor. Even then, without the P&L scoreboard, it is often difficult to know how well they are doing— and why.

By now it should be obvious that P&L plays a valuable role in business and industry. Voluntary enterprise does not have this effective tool. The P&L not only shows the total organization how well it is doing in quantitative terms; it is also a management tool that can influence the length and breadth of the enterprise.

Management Implications

So, what do you do? If yours is not a profit-seeking organization, you do not have P&L with which to monitor operational effectiveness. Is there anything you can do to compensate for this lack, to substitute for it?

First, recognize that you may often develop effective alternatives to P&L. With its emphasis on the service-providing system, a voluntary enterprise often neglects its resource-providing system. In fund-raising you have a counterpart to the profit and loss of business. The business cost versus revenue relationship is similar to the funds raised versus cost of raising funds in voluntary enterprises. The end sought is money contributed, which is just as measurable as profit. The means used to raise the funds are also relatively identifiable and measurable. However, a management system that is primarily attuned to the service-providing aspects of the organization might not take advantage of P&L as a management tool to the degree it can. Recognize that in fund-raising, P&L can serve much the same purpose as it does in a typical profit-seeking enterprise.

This holds true for any part of the enterprise that is "profitized." If some aspect of the organization is currently operating (or could be operated) as if it were a private business, then P&L benefits can apply by operating as if it were in the private sector (for example, a museum gift shop, a church kindergarten, a hospital coffee shop, an educational organization's publications, an art gallery's frame shop, or a fraternal order's paraphernalia and supply service). It applies to where an institution invests its surplus—real estate, the money market, or stocks and bonds. Management can identify all aspects of its enterprise that might function as business operations, and can utilize P&L methodology to advantage.

With the aspects of the organization that can take advantage of P&L objectives isolated, the leadership can give its attention to compensating for its lack in the balance of its operations. Here you are faced with the difficult task of defining objectives, allocating available resources to the various means of reaching these objectives, and measuring efficiency and effectiveness of the performance of the various units and individuals in the organization. Faced with a complicated job of substituting something else for P&L, the not-for-profit leader must select the best from among the alternatives at his disposal. Management should seek to reduce the uncertainty, the softness, the mushiness, and the fuzziness to whatever degree possible. The manager must develop substitutes for the P&L measure as a tool in problem analysis, in decision making, and in his control system. Imperfect as they might be, such substitutes will reduce rationalization and will create an environment in which more positive and crisp management can function.

To do this, there must be clear-cut organizational purposes and a long-range plan including a hierarchy of priorities, some sort of strategic context, and mutually agreed-upon objectives. These objectives should be unambiguous and—if at all possible—should be stated in quantifiable terms. To a degree, quantifiable objectives can serve in lieu of the P&L measure. But, given the tendency of voluntary enterprises to accumulate multiple objectives, there is still the problem of comparison of internal values. Nevertheless, some degree of measurable objectives is a step toward the benefits business enjoys with P&L.

Measurable objectives also provide a discipline that can go a long way toward compensating for the traditional thought processes of voluntary enterprises. Usually, personnel have not been educated and socialized in the attitudes and behaviors common to business management. They have been weak in thinking in terms of results rather than intentions. Substituting measurable objectives, whenever possible, will tighten up the management process.

In the planning function, particularly in forecasting, budgeting, and evaluating activities, measurable objectives can often substitute for P&L. While one recognizes the measurement difficulties discussed in Chapter 3, relative and interim measurements can be developed and applied to the attainment of specific plans. In time, their use will bring to the enterprise some of the advantages that the P&L discipline brings to business and industry.

In the staffing function, substitute measurements of productivity will assist in the training and upgrading of both volunteers and professional staff. They will tend to make the training more specific to the needs of the enterprise and will also tend to motivate the personnel, giving them targets at which to aim. As contributors become more and more sophisticated in their understanding of voluntary enterprise effectiveness, they will inquire more and more about cost-effectiveness in reaching predicted goals and objectives.

The use of some system of measurable objectives will have a positive affect on the guiding, motivation, and direction of personnel. The attainment of objectives will become a motivator, a reinforcer of positive accomplishment, and a means of rewarding productivity. To a lesser degree, it can contribute to cost-effectiveness and efficiency.

Though there is not yet a means of allocating resources between the service-providing system and the resource-producing system that can compare to the profit measure, progress is being made. At a minimum, the leadership of a voluntary enterprise must be aware of the need for equitable and progressive coordination between the two systems. We will spend more time on this in the next chapter, but it is the lack of the P&L measure that makes it the difficulty that it is.

The nature of the voluntary sector denies it the full benefit of the P&L tool of the profit-seeking sector. But by understanding the role it plays in business, voluntary enterprise management can discover ways of improving their organization's effectiveness.

Conclusion

Voluntary enterprises do not have a bottom line in the sense that profit-seeking enterprises do, for the bottom line is the amount of profit or loss. In a business, the profit motive pervades the organization. The part each component of the organization plays in producing that bottom line can be (and is) used as a management tool to expand and improve the business. The customer is constantly expressing his opinion to the company by his purchases and his preferences. This sends a series of messages to the organization, which it passes on to its components. If the messages are read correctly, modifications are made. The result is an automatic evolutionary process of organizational selective adaptation.

Voluntary enterprises do not have this mechanism for selective adaption. They have more difficulty in relating inputs to outputs. Inability to reach an initial goal often results in outright failure or in goal modification. Without P&L as a means of monitoring organizational effectiveness, it is difficult to change only the ineffective aspects of the program. In business, P&L provides feedback. It makes comparisons possible across organizations, among organizations, across departments and branches, and between individuals. It guides it in its competition with external forces and provides a means for internal competition for resources. It facilitates cost-effectiveness and pricing, and it helps employees relate their jobs to the outputs of the business.

The managers of voluntary enterprises have the benefits of P&L in their fund-raising systems. They may also utilize it in aspects of the organization that can operate like a business. Otherwise, they can only develop substitutes. While these substitutes may not function as well as the P&L measure does in business, they can be highly valuable in monitoring operational effectiveness.

The most obvious substitute is a set of quantifiable objectives. Chosen carefully to measure as well as possible the things that reflect the purposes of the enterprise, quantifiable objectives can accomplish for the organization some of the things that P&L does for its business counterparts.

11

POLITICS AND DIPLOMACY

"I learned my politics at the museum," said Nelson Rockefeller.[76] This major figure in state and national government was speaking of the Museum of Modern Art, in which his mother played a prominent role.

Senator George McGovern once told me, "There is no way anyone can function effectively in a voluntary organization without some knowledge of diplomatic or political skills. That is really what it is all about."[77]

Voluntary enterprises have constituencies, contributors, staff, board members, and clients mingling together in an open system. These groups and individuals have a variety of goals and needs. *Voluntary enterprise management requires more diplomacy than in business, where management has more autonomy.* Authority and accountability in most profit-seeking concerns are normally spelled out more precisely than in the voluntary sector. Power is usually more diffused and is not often vested in the upper management echelons of the not-for-profit sector to the degree that it is in business and industry.

Pressures within the constituencies at a given time may run counter to what is objectively best for the organization. While business certainly has its "political" aspects, management decisions more often can be based on clear-cut criteria and less on the characteristic "political" process of many voluntary enterprises. In voluntary enterprises, a great deal of power lies in the lower echelons. In a real sense, voluntary enterprises are "governed." They have many political aspects requiring the exercise of considerable diplomacy on the part of management.

I discussed the characteristic with Moon Landrieu shortly after President Carter had named him Secretary of Housing and Urban Development. He agreed with my basic premise but reaffirmed that you can never completely remove "politics and personalities" from management in the private sector. The secretary, who had just left the private sector

116

to accept a public sector appointment, added, "However, the larger the private sector organization grows, the more political it becomes."[78]

The voluntary organization tends to be democratic in nature, so all factions may express themselves through political processes. Resources are voluntarily contributed and produced by persuasion, so continued support is dependent on concurrence with management direction. Leadership, to a great extent, is based upon the consent of the participants. Voluntary enterprise leaders serve at the pleasure of their constituency, so the political nature of their job is inescapable. The effectiveness of the organization is often perceived subjectively instead of measured precisely. The use of diplomacy and persuasion plays a significant role. Subordinates may bypass hierarchical superiors or appeal to internal constituencies, so managers lack some of the authority of their business counterparts. Therefore, a degree of political adroitness in addition to management competence is required of staff members. The manager must add a political sensitivity to his professional expertise—an ability to form coalitions, to marshall support, and to inspire confidence. The manager must be a leader.

Political Considerations

A voluntary enterprise not only serves as a vehicle for achieving certain cooperative goals but also provides a means for career advancement for its paid professionals. This is true of any organization, no matter the sector. As in any other organization, decisions are sometimes made for objective-oriented reasons, and sometimes for reasons having more to do with personalities in power. Because the currency of many such organizations is recognition and influence rather than dollars and cents, the political aspects are prominent. Since organizations provide a framework for the exercise of power, this fact should be honestly faced and acknowledged. A frank recognition of interpersonal interplay will help create a realistic climate. It will help avoid the elaborate creation of an illusion that everything is done in a sterile, computerlike environment of rationalism.

Is the political nature of the voluntary enterprise good or bad? Is the requirement that the manager be skilled in diplomacy a positive or a negative factor? Does the lack of a more direct-line autonomy make for a better or a worse kind of organization? These questions may be debated, but it makes no difference what you conclude—they remain an integral part of the nature of the creature.

Among the positive aspects of a voluntary enterprise are its democratic nature, its potential for openness and fairness, its emphasis on human qualities, and its tendency toward greater community involvement.

Consider the values of its democratic nature. As Moon Landrieu said, "It is sometimes bothersome, but a very necessary good."[79] Voluntary enterprises provide a forum where individuals with a common concern about the purposes of the organization can arrive at a consensus through discussion and debate. Assuming that the process works, it can ultimately result in the survival of the best services that the constituency is willing to support. Since the constituency gives its allegiance voluntarily, a great deal of freedom is available for expression and contribution.

Working in such an open environment encourages both paid and voluntary leadership to reflect on what they are doing. Constraints and accountability reinforce equity and fairness and encourage open communication. Political feasibility mandates a context of sharing, concern for dissenting opinions, and a desire for harmony. As a rule, voluntary organizations have a commitment to participation-involvement and individual freedom. Their expressive nature encourages the individual to help with problem solving and decision making. Their democratic process emphasizes human values and provides opportunities for personal growth, self-fulfillment, interaction, comradeship, informality, and spontaneous expression.

Community involvement in the life of the organization, and of the organization in the community, is part and parcel of its political dependency. There is concern for the public interest in most of these organizations. Because of its need for third-party resource contributions, there is considerable communication with both individuals and groups outside of its specific membership.

Another aspect, considered a "plus" by many, is the opportunity they provide for involvement by those who simply enjoy political activity. Indeed, many work willingly and well because of the incentives for leadership afforded by these organizations. Many who would never run for any public office point with pride to their trophies of success in the political milieu of organizational life.

But the negative aspects of the political nature of voluntary enterprises are many. They are particularly onerous to the task-oriented leaders who would like to manage their organization for maximum results. Many who would succeed in the business world but are committed to a not-for-profit purpose see the diplomatic demands as a time-consuming burden. They define "political" in negative terms, and engage in it with a sense of being tainted. Indeed, many of the positive features from the point of view of a relatively casual volunteer are a pain in the rear for the professional who depends on success for advancement in his career. So consider now some negative aspects.

In a political context, there is a temptation to respond to the lowest common denominator. An unhappy client who receives free services can create more problems than a business customer who pays for his. A frustrated member, contributor, or volunteer worker with "connections" can stop the organizational machinery. Forward progress, no matter how well conceived, will leave someone behind; the few left behind can cause many to have second thoughts. The very framework for encouraging the realization of personal goals and self-expression can become highly disruptive in a political environment. If the organization's vision is not matched by maturity of judgment and courage, much energy can be dissipated in placating activity.

More so than its profit-seeking counterpart, the voluntary enterprise is subject to a "squeaking wheel gets the grease" climate. Its political nature can encourage the unsure to respond to losers rather than winners, to self-seekers rather than true altruists, and to soft fuzzyheads instead of realists with ideals.

Indeed, there are members with organizations who object to the organization's doing its best. (They would not so state their feelings, but they enjoy an atmosphere of inefficiency and failure, perhaps because it cloaks their own inadequacies.) An emphasis on professionalism in management represents a threat—even when the professionalism is designed to complement rather than compete with volunteerism. They feel such progress will kill the human qualities they enjoy, water down the opportunity for self-expression, and inhibit freedom and participation.

The political interplay of forces often reveals that the lines of responsibility and accountability are not clear. The board (which presumably represents the source of power) does not always hold the lines of power—or sometimes it holds too much. In some cases, the chief executive officer holds the power. In some, all the shots are called by a major funding source that sees the organization simply as its agent. The "spiritual" or philosophical leader who symbolizes the ideals on which the organization is built might not be in the official chain of command at all. In business the stockholders have the ultimate authority (which in practice they exercise only in time of crisis). But in voluntary enterprises it can be difficult for the management to determine to whom they are ultimately accountable. The seat of power can shift from time to time, as in any political entity.

Another negative aspect from management's point of view is that

the manager cannot always exercise full authority over the various elements within the system for which he is responsible. He rarely has a
tight, clear-cut, and responsive structure through which he can work in
meeting his predetermined objectives.

George McGovern used the term *command function*.[80] "You don't
have a command function in a voluntary organization," he said. "You
and I can't function as generals. We've got to function with the voluntary commitment of the people that we are trying to lead, and that
requires a considerably larger measure of diplomatic skills . . . than any
other thing that people are doing."

Pity the poor voluntary enterprise executive who seeks to carry out
policy set by the board, but who finds that the political wind changes
between board meetings. It is common in certain types of associations
for the organization to become an arena for combat among constituent
bodies. Again quoting Moon Landrieu:

> I have talked with individuals who have worked in political, nonprofit, and
> profit-making organizations, and inevitably found the lines of authority
> within the profit-making organizations much clearer. They had more autono-
> my. The line of authority was much more direct.[81]

The business organization enjoys more continuity of leadership.
The voluntary enterprise, by its very nature, has elections, often at
several levels. Leadership positions must be passed around. Election to
office is a reward and an incentive for others. Unqualified persons often
are elected to high and influential positions. This can have a disruptive
influence and can lead to short-term rather than strategic planning. It
can lead to a disruption of the implementation of plans as each new
regime seeks to put its stamp on the program. If the elected officers
exercise significant power and derive benefits from staying in office,
they could be more concerned with being reelected than with substantial
organizational success.

In a political environment, perception plays a greater role than reality. When this factor is added to the difficulty that voluntary enterprises
already face because of their measurability problems, it can add up to a
surplus of self-deception. So the way the organization sees itself is of
great importance.

Managers in voluntary enterprises must be accessible to their constituency. This cannot be delegated. They may try, but the attempt by
no means will necessarily be accepted. And if the accessibility is delegated, there will be a strong drain of political power from the delegate to
the delegatee. In my seminars on time-management and delegation, I
see that the accessibility that nonprofit managers must maintain is a
serious encroachment on the control of their time. The better sense of

"ownership" and identity with the organization they are able to develop, the more accessible they must be. When they seek to carve out blocks of time in which to do what they alone can do best, they are vulnerable to criticism for their aloofness. But, as McGovern said in our discussion, the voluntary enterprise managers must "be sensitive to other people's needs . . . to know what turns people on, and what excites them."[82]

Another negative element of the political aspect is the wide range of groups that must be considered at each decision-making fork in the road. This slows down the process and makes it more complex and difficult. Not only must management consider various pressure groups who are basically aligned with their general direction, they must also consider the opposition. In this type of organization, you cannot fire your opponents. You can sometimes shift them around. You can encourage them to go elsewhere. You can try to appease them. If they pose a really serious threat, you can try Cardinal Richelieu's advice: "First, all means to conciliate; failing that, all means to crush."[83] But you cannot fire them. An opposition party can be an asset to an organization, keeping it responsive and disciplined, but this is little consolation to the manager in power.

In this kind of organizational milieu, some things must be done that are nonproductive for the organization but that are politically necessary. The constituency must be pleased. Favors must be done. Perceptions must be altered. Feathers must be unruffled and smoothed down. Power blocks must be placated. Even a paid manager with a contract must be "reelected" with support from those elsewhere in the organization's structure. If the manager's leadership is good for the organization and he wants to be around to do more good, he will occasionally do some things that are not as good as others. The manager must trade one thing for another, negotiate, bargain, be alert to internal and external "public opinion," and in dozens of other ways exercise "the art of the possible." Whether it be to build personal support for better public relations or to counter opposing forces, he has a lot of politically necessary but otherwise nonproductive activity.

Which brings us to the fact that the managers of voluntary enterprises are subject to much public scrutiny. As open as they are, there is little they do that escapes the view of either internal or external groups. In spite of interest in the internal workings of large private corporations, they remain in less of a goldfish bowl than voluntary enterprises. Management is somewhat inhibited by being able to keep few secrets, and by being subject to outside monitoring. This is not to say that anything illegal or immoral is going on. It persists with problems in dealing with the competition, and even outside voices can influence internal matters. The manager of an organization that is supposed to provide some sort of societal good is in a poor position to say to anyone, "It's none of your business!" Public scrutiny may also bring unhealthy pressures to show quick visible results when indeed the organization might need strategies with long-term payoffs.

Public scrutiny is closely akin to high public expectations. The revelation of a homosexual relationship of a youth and his coach is much more newsworthy than the same relationship within a business context. Catch an embezzler at a university and it affects contributions to the endowment, and a stigma becomes part of the institution's historical legacy. Studies show that citizens expect greater integrity, accountability, and justice from nonprofit organizations than they do from business.[84] After all, these are the institutions that raise funds by appealing to higher motives. They challenge us to do our best, and teach us our moral and ethical standards. Why shouldn't the public expect more and better things from the very organizations that point us onward and upward? Unfortunately, in spite of grandiose titles and trappings, they are operated by people, like everything else.

Leadership Implications

I have already touched on some management concerns resulting from the political aspects of voluntary enterprises, and some of the demands for political acumen and diplomatic finesse. But how do you learn the appropriate skills? Do you major in political science? Do you sign up for a crash course? I suggest first that you recognize that the new science of management is but an extension of the old art of government. Second, I suggest you find a worthy mentor who will serve as a model and lead you through the labyrinth and explain what is happening along the way. Third, I recommend massive doses of experience, with ample mistakes that you make only once. There is nothing to equal getting caught in a bear trap to teach you how to recognize one.

Early on, a person in a leadership position will recognize that his purpose is to apply power to some end. To have power and not exercise it toward some worthy objective is to waste a valuable resource. A leader gets into the seat of power and remains there because of his ability to effect a coalition of forces that endow him with the opportunity to call the shots to a mutual advantage. The greater his competence to produce, the more potent is his ability to hold the coalition together.

The political nature affects the policy-making process—decision making at all levels—and it can be time-consuming and require that as much energy be spent on personnel and human-relations matters as on providing the service for which the organization exists. A good manager will seek to lead the enterprise to take full advantage of the positive aspects of the democratic process and minimize its counterproductive side. The tradition of group decision making in the voluntary sector is congruent with our American concern for freedom of choice and the right of dissent. It is different from top-down decision making, and it gives the constituency a sense of participation, cohesion, and ownership of organizational goals. However, when the need for the group-decision process is added to the difficulty of measuring outputs, making the right decisions is most difficult.

I recommend to any voluntary enterprise that uses a structured planning process that they insert an additional step. When I have consulted with organizational leadership dealing with the planning function, I have suggested that this step be added just prior to final adoption of plans. I call it simply *response prediction.* It is the activity of assessing the response of the constituency to any change, and of considering the potential political consequences. By building this activity into the process, the leadership will deal with the realities and possible consequences of their actions.

When the management has adopted its plans and moves into establishing the organization required to implement them, I recommend two additional steps. The first is a preliminary informing of the constituents of any organizational changes. The second is a review of their response to the change. These activities are not to be confused with a trial-and-error approach. I do not suggest that you test a series of organization modifications until one of them fits. It is like floating a trial weather balloon, a circuit breaker in an electronic system, or a shear pin on an outboard motor—a deliberate weak point in the system. It is designed into the system for the rare but dangerous circumstance. A brief time lag is allowed between the step of informing and the step of reviewing the response. It provides a brief pause to test the wind before the relatively irreversible forward momentum begins. Several recent U.S. Presidents have used a similar, if less forthright, technique. Prior to the official announcement of a contemplated action, the intention is "leaked" to the press. If the public responds well, the official proclamation ensues. If there is a sufficiently hostile outcry, no action is taken, and the "leak" is dismissed as an erroneous rumor. It is a political means of testing the water before taking the plunge.

General consensus is essential. Without it, the cohesive glue dissolves. Few voluntary enterprises have assets sufficient to begin anew and build a new constituency. Few managers survive a split that sends even a significant minority out on a tangent. Yet the enterprise will not keep pace with the society, much less make real progress, if the machinery halts every time opposition is registered. The optimum is achieved by a balance between task accomplishment and constituency sensitivity.

Studies show that a good manager is one who has a deep concern for both human relations and task accomplishment.[85] Both the output of the organization and the expressive needs of its members are given serious weight. Those perceived as average are the ones who stress task to the neglect of people. Howard Foshee, a senior manager in the largest Protestant denomination, the Southern Baptists, has given this balance much thought. He said to me: "The good manager must be an individual who understands both his leadership role and his servant role. He must lead the organization toward clearly set-out goals, and he must help persons to achieve their own ideals and expectations." He paused, then added, "Diplomacy demands an understanding of the use of power."[86]

An effective manager needs power. This is both an internal psychological need within his personality and an external pragmatic need for doing his job. It is a driving force and a tool of the trade. French and Raven see power as coming from five different sources:[87]

1. *Reward power* stems from the number of positive rewards (money, protection, and such) that people perceive a potential leader can muster.
2. *Coercive power* stems from the perceived expectations of people that punishment (being fired, reprimanded, or such) will follow if one does not comply with the aims of a potential leader.
3. *Legitimate power* develops from internalized values that dictate that a leader has a legitimate right to influence and that one has an obligation to accept this influence.
4. *Reference power* is based on the identification of people with a potential leader and what that leader stands for or symbolizes.
5. *Expert power* results from a potential leader having expertise or knowledge in an area in which that leader wants to influence others.

The ability of the manager to apply power effectively to the legitimate organizational purposes will depend on how well he works with his own group, his inner circle. He must consolidate his power, from whatever source, in a relationship with a select group. As the central figure in the group, the manager utilizes it as an aid to problem analysis, in decision making, in the implementation of his program, in the evaluation of performance, and in sensing the pulse of the larger constituency. An article in the *Harvard Business Review*[88] points out that this power-wielding group need not even involve the executive with his immediate subordinates. "It may indeed bypass the second level as in the case of the Presidents of the United States who do not build confident relationships within their cabinets, but instead rely on members of the executive staff or on selected individuals outside the formal apparatus."

I agree that there needs to be a consolidation of power around a central figure. But that central figure must not be so restricted by the group that he loses touch with the larger organization. Witness one President whose inner circle was like a cocoon. He was insulated from reality by it, and his concern for its survival led to his downfall, and to serious injury to the nation.

How conflicts are resolved is important in a voluntary enterprise. The manager must never forget the voluntary nature of the organization. The bonds that bind contributors, volunteer workers, and staff together are often dependent on strong affiliation. A minor disagreement at any level can easily escalate and cause a major rift. The folklore of virtually every organization contains a case of such a rift. Everyone remembers the bad feelings, the lengthy fallout, the deep scars. Often no one can remember the issue that precipitated it.

In a business organization, disagreements can be handled arbitrarily by the superior of the persons involved. He can use control sanctions, such as dismissal, transfer, or witholding of promotion. But these controls are not always available in a voluntary enterprise. Consensus is important. The democratic process must be preserved. Goodwill, harmony, and a perception of enthusiastic striving toward goals is highly valuable. Whether the organization structures diversity or works toward a reduction of diversity, it should predetermine a procedure for conflict resolution that will isolate the specific case and protect the cohesion and integrity of the large organization.

The political context adds a dimension to the organization's formal public relations program. Its initial focus is probably on either the public from which its resources are drawn or the public to which it provides its services. Its immediate payoff is seen in contributed dollars, volunteer or member recruitment, and a favorable image to the recipients of services. But it must also be congruent with the perceptions of those within the organization, and consistent with their motivations.

These are some of the implications for managing voluntary enterprises that grow out of its need for diplomacy. Management lacks the autonomy found in most profit-seeking enterprises, and its need for

voluntarism and for maintaining the support of its constituency produces a political environment. This in turn often leads the organization
to develop multiple purposes to satisfy the needs of diverse groups. This
we will discuss in the next chapter.

Conclusion

Voluntary enterprises are political organizations in which individuals and groups vie for influence and position. Part of their purpose
is to achieve some goal through the instrumentality of the democratic
process. In order to elicit the energy of the organization, harness it, and
help guide it, the manager must be skilled in diplomacy. He does not
usually have the autonomy of his business counterpart, so his interpersonal, persuasive, and motivational skills are essential to successful
leadership.

This gives the organizational format a number of advantages. The
enterprises are democratic and open, and emphasize human qualities.
On the other side of the coin, the manager has less direct means for
getting results; human relations will often override task attainment. As a
result, the manager must have a wide range of skills in the exercise of
power if he is to strike an effective balance.

12

MULTIPLE PURPOSES

Voluntary enterprises often have trouble defining their purpose because they usually have more than one.

To begin with, they usually have an expressive purpose on behalf of their constituency and an instrumental purpose for their clients. But this is rarely the end of their purpose collecting. They initially delivered a service to certain clients in a specific location. Inevitably someone notes that with the same delivery system the organization could meet other needs in the same location or for the same clients. Another arrow is added to their quiver. Or rather, they add another bull's-eye for the number of arrows already in the quiver.

Voluntary enterprises tend to accumulate multiple purposes. A business may enlarge its product line or expand its services in order to maximize its profits. But its organizational purpose remains the same: to provide a return on investments by producing a profit. For example, one company began as an oil royalty company, buying royalties from landowners and profiting from oil production. Three years later, they modified their activity and began exploring for oil and gas on their own. Later, they began operating gravel and sand pits. The company was involved in three different activities, but all were for the purpose of making money. But as a voluntary enterprise utilizes an existing organization to meet new needs, its initial purpose is modified or expanded.

Organizations in the voluntary sector have an even more dramatic option. They can change their entire purpose. The classic example is the March of Dimes. The National Foundation for Infantile Paralysis instituted a massive campaign against polio. With the support of President Franklin D. Roosevelt, mothers and others solicited the entire nation. The dimes became dollars, and eventually the organization succeeded! A cure was found for polio. But in reaching its goal, it faced its own demise. In eliminating polio, Dr. Jonas Salk also eliminated the need for the organization. But they had offices, loyal employees, and a good fund-raising structure. No problem; they simply found a new purpose to utilize the talents of the organization. As the National Foundation, they now work against birth defects.

Why Accumulate Purposes?

Voluntary enterprises tend to fall into two categories. Instrumental organizations exist for some societal purpose. Expressive ones serve the needs of their members. But even those that are primarily instrumental often have an expressive side. In order to recruit and retain volunteers, there has to be some satisfaction or fun in volunteering. To compete for capable volunteers, the organization must give some attention to their needs. So an expressive purpose is added to the instrumental purpose. The workers' need to work and the givers' need to give is matched by the need of the organization to provide opportunities for satisfaction, personal actualization, socializing, or recognition.

Additional purposes are added to maximize the use of the delivery capability of the enterprise. With the same management, the same re-source-attraction system, and a few modifications in the service-provid-ing system, an entirely new need can be met. When this factor coincides with the real or perceived needs of the clients, the enterprise is under pressure to match its capacity with the need and move into an additional field. The desire for growth and the economies of scale and the synergy in many such circumstances make the adding of additional purposes inevitable.

For example, consider an adult education program with which I was involved in Pakistan. Its original purpose was to teach illiterate adults to read. Seeing that an effective literacy education component would en-hance its own program, a large agricultural development center offered its ample campus as an operational base. The director of the literacy project concentrated her efforts among the women for two reasons. First, literate wives and mothers were known to have a multiplying effect on literacy, spreading it to their families. Second, women in the province had long been suppressed, and the director saw literacy as the first step upward for the female population.

Gaining confidence with their newfound knowledge, the women began to seek other ways of improving their lot. After learning to read, several of the women students requested assistance from the literacy program director. They needed seed money to buy cloth, which they planned to dye and sew to manufacture inexpensive saris, the graceful flowing dress of that part of the world. The same agricultural development center offered a vacant building and a number of long tables. My organization in New York was approached for the initial capital and for permission to allocate some of the time of the literacy program personnel to help the women get started. The permission was granted. The sari factory thrived from the outset. I saw it in operation myself on a visit a year later, and learned that its success had led to the addition of another component to the total rural development of the province. Our response to the women's request built up sufficient trust that the women were now willing to attend family-planning clinics that they had previously boycotted.

I remember an urban center, designed to provide recreation for black youths, that was adjacent to an area inundated by Vietnamese refugees in the early 1970s. The Area Agency on Aging was looking for a facility to meet some of the needs of the older Vietnamese. The recreation center sought and got funds for a new wing to their building and added an entirely new component to their organization.

In service organizations, the market demand is often huge in relation to the supply. In meeting one need, the staff and volunteers are exposed to other needs. In the midst of trying to work themselves out of one job, they encounter two more that their organization could handle as their constituents plead, "if only we. . . ." Little by little, the range of concerns widens. As the scope of services expands, purposes are modified and new ones are added.

Susan Ellis, a consultant to volunteer groups, expressed it well when she told me: "Often the clients you are working with are multiproblem clients. There is no such thing as the pure delinquent who has delinquency as his or her only concern. They are often also illiterate, need medical care, and are undernourished. After a certain period of time, an organization living in this atmosphere of constant need begins to expand almost in self-defense."[89]

Another reason why voluntary enterprises accumulate additional purposes is their response to opportunities of additional resources. Federal funds are suddenly available to teach English to the foreign-born, and the organization already has a used-clothing outlet in a Spanish-speaking neighborhood. Grants for drug abuse dry up as funds for women in transition are opened. So terminology is changed, programs are modified, and proposals are prepared to respond to a new opportunity. A foundation will not help you build a library in Hong Kong, but it has been looking for an organization to distribute high-protein fish meal in the Orient. A summer camp for girls in the mountains is approached by a volunteer who will conduct a two-week portrait-painting workshop. The board member and major contributor to an organization fostering more cooperation between religion and the arts is looking for someone to administer a fund to use the arts to open a broader world to handicapped children. A national organization helping people with pre-retirement planning gradually responds to an opportunity to own its own mutual insurance company. The wife of the director of an expensive day care center knows sign language, so an evening class is offered to deaf people new to the city. Large and small, services and purposes are accumulated.

Organizational personnel contribute to added purposes. Survival needs and empire building contribute their share of additional programs and purposes. Both staff and volunteer personnel have a vested interest in the success of the enterprise. They must justify their relationship, and justify the existence of the organization. They may wish to diversify, widen its scope, enlarge its size, adapt to trends, expand into new areas. This need of individuals is not different from what you find in the profit-seeking sector. The end sought is the same: a future for the enterprise, with an attractive place in it for the individual.

Akin to this is another need many voluntary enterprises can provide—the opportunity to particpate in matters of importance and a wide range of influential public issues and affairs. Voluntary enterprise leaders often have more opportunity for influence, public exposure, impact, and notoriety than their business counterparts. (Many persons in commerce and industry find that the time they devote to voluntary positions in not-for-profit organizations feeds their ego more than their often prosaic paid positions.) This need may draw an organization into advocacy and other purposes.

Howard Foshee, of the Southern Baptist Convention, reminded me that voluntary enterprises attract particularly dedicated, concerned, and conscientious individuals. "They are persons with idealistic natures . . . generally achievers and goal-oriented," he said. "They have innovative, inventive, and creative minds, and are constantly looking for new ways to serve. If their leaders do not call them back to their central purpose, their goals will go off in all directions."[90]

Political realities generate additional purposes. I asked Max Wortman, former president of the Academy of Management, about this. He responded: "You may have ten or twenty different viewpoints in an organization. In order to get support for your special interest, you may have to support the interests of others. You ultimately end up with a lot of different purposes. It's primarily a political thing."[91]

Aspects of Multiplicity

For whatever reason, voluntary enterprises tend to accumulate multiple purposes. The motives and mechanics of adding services are quite similar to those of the profit-seeking sector, but the end is different. A business retains its profit target. It adds arrows to its quiver and may increase its ability to hit its targets. A voluntary enterprise adds targets and quite possibly decreases its probability of getting its arrows into the bull's-eye.

The positive facet is that such organizations can be adaptable and responsive to a variety of needs. Each time an existing purpose is modified or a new purpose added, a need is being met. It might be the need of an individual to express one of his concerns. It could meet the need of a funding entity for an agent to apply resources to specific recipients. Or it could be feeding some hunger in the lives of a client population. The voluntary sector's flexibility and diversity allows a tremendous amount of energy to be tapped and applied to needs. Often a single organization can be a conduit from that reservoir to several points of need. This allows many targets to have an opportunity of getting a share of the arrows.

There are a variety of negative facets to this characteristic. The greater the number of targets, the greater the difficulties for the archer. Among the negative aspects are the resultant overextended supply lines, the incongruity of stated goals with *ad hoc* circumstances, conflicts among purposes, a lack of unified thrust, and a maintenance orientation.

With multiple purposes, management often finds that the organization's supply lines become overextended. As with Napoleon, deep into Russia and far from France, supplies could prove inadequate. As with Napoleon, overextension could so tax the enterprise that it collapses upon itself. If the leadership does not act, it could collapse because it outruns its resources, which are stretched like a rubber band beyond the breaking point. It could collapse like a frail bridge because the organization is inadequate to handle the traffic. It could collapse like a punctured balloon because the demands of overserviced, underserved clients are too great for it to handle. It could collapse like a stack of children's blocks because time runs out before all the services can be performed.

Also there can be an incongruity of stated goals with *ad hoc* circumstances. Often the original purpose or official goals of the organization have been left behind as more and more priority is given to new ones. As circumstances change with time, and more resources are allocated to one purpose than to another, the organization's actual activities drift away from its officially stated purposes. This is not to say that anything is wrong with the changed direction. But when the official position of the group is not correspondingly modified, there can be confusion (or even deception).

Purposes can come into conflict with each other. Those charged with the responsibility for carrying out the programs may get mixed signals from those who set policy. The board's mandates might confuse the staff. There might not be enough time to attend to the various purposes within the allotted time. One purpose could have the backing of part of the constituency, and another the support of another faction. Some members of the organization could bear allegiance to it because of their commitment to only one purpose. They will support it and fight for it—perhaps to the disadvantage of the larger organization. If such alignments become widespread, the organization loses its unity and becomes an unstable coalition.

In larger complex enterprises the conflict between purposes can move outside of the organizational borders. For example, a senior-adult program might oppose a city ordinance to open a recreation center, while a youth project, sponsored by the same organization, supports the ordinance.

No enterprise would deliberately plan purposes that will compete destructively either internally or externally. But time and expansion can cause conflicting purposes to evolve. For example, consider a new trade association. At the outset, it searches for worthy purposes to justify its existence, to attract support from its constituent organizations, and to give it a sense of magnitude. Within a few years, 12 of its original 16 programs are surviving. Each does a good job of providing services. Demand for the various services grows. As the organization grows, each program changes shape slightly. With the passage of time and continued demand, there is more growth and modification in response to demand. It is at this point that conflicts become evident, and conflict resolution becomes more difficult.

Multiple purposes can blunt the unified thrust of an enterprise. You cannot build the fires of emotion and enthusiasm with multiple purposes as well as with a single sharp purpose. Good marketing becomes difficut. The position of the organization is hard for the potential contributor to identify. Potential volunteers get vague or confused signals. New members of the constituency are unsure of what they are buying into. Forward movement becomes tentative. One member does not immediately identify other members as having the same motivation and mission as himself. There is a lack of the kind of certainty, focus, and common concern that builds strong cohesive ties and a willingness to sacrifice for the cause.

The lack of focus on a single cause (or cluster of closely aligned causes) leads to another negative aspect. If you are not a part of the organization because of a clearly defined cause or goal, then why are you supporting it? If the purposes are so diverse as to be fuzzy, your dedication must be to the organization itself—the mechanism, the structure, the conduit that operates to achieve the various ends. Such a motive lacks the compelling power of a cause outside of and beyond the organization. It tends to cause a slowing down of the machinery itself. Instead of applying energy toward the external goal, the group expends its energy on maintaining the organization. The enterprise can become the end instead of the means. Energy is concentrated on static maintenance of the organization. Methodology and tradition become goals. This maintenance orientation can be a prelude to death, for it lacks any real means of attracting new adherents.

Implications for Management

The tendency of voluntary enterprises to accumulate multiple purposes challenges management to develop an optimum mix while still avoiding the pitfalls. Like an archer, he must select attractive and attainable targets within the range of his bow, with the assurance that his quiver has enough arrows.

The key is in the planning function. It begins with an evaluation of the posture of the organization in relation to what it wants to become. Before objectives are selected there must be a forecast of alternative futures. The forecast must consider both the organization and its environment as it seeks to predict the range of circumstances that could ensue. The existence of multiple purposes, and proposals for new ones, will be unavoidably evident when the time for preparing objectives comes. It is at this point that more can be done to properly handle multiple objectives than at any other.

When an organization has multiple purposes (or many major subheads to a unified purpose), it is essential that all be clearly identified and acknowledged. This is especially important for voluntary enterprises with expressive as well as instrumental ends. Many tend to state their instrumental but not their expressive objectives, sometimes ignoring the existence of the expressive. This hypocrisy will fill the entire management process with confusion. There will be ambiguity between official statements and the "unwritten" laws. For example, I once met with a women's organization that had undertaken as its project the provision of thousands of layettes for babies at a charity hospital. It was a project with a lot of heart and one that met a practical need. Caught up with the idea, and having a friend who manufactured baby clothes, I suggested to the executive committee that we could improve their effectiveness by making a deal with the manufacturer. At approximately the retail cost of material, we could get the finished product. The ladies' faces dropped at the mention of the idea. A lot of meaningless oblique discussion followed. Then, the full impact of my misreading of the situation hit me. Their unwillingness to own up to all of their objectives had pulled me into a trap. My idea was cost-effective. But it would have deprived the women of the joy of sewing the tiny clothes, and of imagining the happiness they would bring to each new mother and child. Expressive objectives are important and real, and they should be clearly stated along with the instrumental ones.

Once the purposes have been clearly identified, a hierarchy of purposes and short- and long-range objectives can be prepared. Ranking purposes and attendant objectives in order by level will prevent many problems, from the board down to the newest direct-service volunteer.

The process of prioritizing purposes and objectives is a valuable exercise in itself. It provides a framework and a concrete way of thinking and talking about the organization. Additional purposes are often uncovered, relations among objectives become evident, posture and directions are clarified, ambiguity is reduced, and problems surface so they can be addressed. Intervening objectives are seen in relationship to those on higher levels in the hierarchy. Cause, effect, and the limitations of individual objectives are better understood. Once such a ranking has been completed, management is well on its way toward an organizational strategy with which to reach its ultimate ends.

Be prepared for disagreements during the process of setting up a hierarchy of purposes. Disagreements likely would occur even among a group of objective-disinterested persons. But with a board composed of persons with their own vested interests, subject to a variety of pressures, differences are inevitable.

Ideally, the process should be undertaken by a truly representative group. If the members of the group have a loyalty to the total organization rather than only to one of its aspects, the exercise can be completed in spite of different opinions and without alienation. Such is the nature of the democratic process. Lest the fear of alienation deter you from undertaking the endeavor, remember that failing to prioritize purposes in the planning function only delays the inevitable. Often a skilled outsider can facilitate the process. Uninvolved in hidden agendas, interpersonal feuds, and vested interests, the objective outsider has the potential for leading the group through the process to an optimum result.

Organizational leadership should be aware of the sources of additional purposes. A board member might wish to assert himself, to contribute ideas, or to make a speech. He could recommend that the organization get in on a burning current issue. A timid staff member might lack the courage to offer counterarguments. Inventive staff members, seeking a bigger slice of the pie for their own interests, are often sources of purposes. Heavy contributors often get a quick response from a lean organization. Clients are another legitimate source of ideas. If management analyzes potential sources of additional purposes and establishes a procedure for adopting (and rejecting) additional ones, the whole matter becomes a managed rather than a random activity.

In the management function of organizing, multiple functions can create complexity. It is a challenge to consolidate like objectives with like objectives, pair like skills with like skills, provide for adequate supervision, and avoid being overextended. If the staff is small, you must avoid too wide a span of control. If a substantial volunteer force is available, they can be utilized to the maximum if the work load is programmed to avoid conflicting schedules. A healthy device that helps avoid an overload of purposes (without unduly squelching innovation) is the acceptance of the new purpose in concept, while making it clear that it cannot be implemented until such time as the resources and organizational capacity have been enlarged sufficiently to handle it effectively.

I personally enjoy working with a multipurpose organization. The fact that the enterprise is not closed to modifying or adding to its purpose makes it dynamic. It stimulates creativity and receptiveness to new thought, and infuses it with vitality. But the same quality challenges the manager to hold tight to the reins, for he rides a spirited steed.

Conclusion

Voluntary enterprises tend to accumulate multiple purposes. This could result in a meandering from its intentional path. There are a variety of reasons for this characteristic. While business survives and expands by modifying its means of producing a profit, a not-for-profit organization might modify its ends in order to grow or survive. It could adapt to satisfy organizational needs, to meet the needs of contributors and volunteers, or to respond to the needs of its constituents or clients.

The capacity to add purposes is positive, in that it allows the organization to be adaptable and responsive to a variety of needs. But it also presents problems: An organization can become overextended, its stated goals could differ from its real ones; it could lack a unified thrust and find itself preoccupied with maintaining the organization rather than with achieving its purposes. Management should take advantage of the creativity and flexibility this characteristic presents. But the primary implication for management is the need to prioritize purposes and set up a hierarchy of objectives. This is an excellent planning tool for dealing with multiple purposes. Purposes should be identified and clearly stated. The leadership should be alert to the sources of its multiple purposes and should take care in organizing to handle the complexity that accompanies this condition.

13

DISTINCTIVE SOCIAL CHARACTER

Durante, Presley, and Caruso—all singers, but each with his own style.

Picasso, Rockwell, and Rembrandt—all painters, but each with his own style.

Bernhardt, Brice, and Hawn—all actresses, but each with her own style.

Individuals have distinctive styles, and groups of individuals have their distinctive social characters. We have long been aware of social character, but the concept was best enunciated by Erich Fromm. He identified it as a cluster of traits, shared by members of an organization or class or nation. Though individuals may deviate from the dominant character, those shared traits determine group values and behavior, which are manifested in feelings, attitudes, and actions. This social character can be modified, but it greatly influences what and how an organization functions.[92]

Voluntary enterprises tend to have a distinctive social character that influences their management style. While this also can be said of two industries or two individual companies, studies have shown that individuals with distinct expectations are motivated to seek employment in the differing business and voluntary sectors. The nature of the two types of organizations places priorities on certain effective styles at various levels. As a class, business managers and voluntary enterprise managers are different breeds of cats, and they effectively manage their organizations in distinctive ways.

The ideological goals, the typically normative compliance structure of voluntary enterprises, and their expressive component influence social character or climate. The more effective leaders often exercise normative influence over paid staff, volunteers, and members. Individuals who determine the expressive ends tend to dominate those concerned with instrumental means. A premium is placed on one's commitment to an ideal, personal charisma, status, character, and ability to facilitate good human relations. Etzioni writes:

> We would expect, for example, that individuals who have leadership qualities, such as persuasive power, vision, ability to verbalize, and the like, would be more inclined to seek a career in normative than in utilitarian organizations, and to prefer a utilitarian organization to a coercive one, since these organizations differ in the opportunities they offer for satisfaction of the need-dispositions associated with leadership qualities.[93]

Imagine a scale representing the work people do, and people who do the work. On one end of this scale are tasks that are routine, specifiable, and long-term. At the other extreme are tasks that are not specifiable, unpredictable, and one of a kind. At the routine end of the scale you find most manufacturing organizations, and at the other, voluntary enterprises (in which most of the people who do the work are professionals with a service motive). These extremes are reflected in the types of people who do the work.

Social character affects the characteristic way an organization works—its pace, its personality, its image, its climate, the way it deals with people, and the emphasis of its activities. It reflects its leaders, its constituency, its traditions, its environment, and what it has found effective in getting certain responses from certain publics under certain circumstances. Consider Delta Airlines as an example of a business posture affecting social character. The attire, attitude, and approach of the personnel reflect crisp, cool professionalism. The gray ladies and candy-stripers at a hospital also wear uniforms but reflect a different social character.

Difference in social character is a matter of degree. It cannot be averaged any more than can individual human personalities. Doubtless you can find some voluntary enterprises with a culture that encourages a more "businesslike" style than a typical business. But certain social characters do tend to be characteristic of the two sectors. Awareness of the differences can be valuable.

Characteristic Appeal and Individualism

The not-for-profit purpose influences culture. Persons interested in profit are drawn to business to a greater degree than they are to voluntary enterprises. While many business leaders idealistically dedicate themselves to goals that transcend their companies, they are first of all responsible for producing a profit. Idealists and persons with a strong dedication to a cause tend to gravitate to appropriate not-for-profit organizations. Persons interested in certain specialties are drawn to organizations in their fields of interest: educators to schools, social workers to social agencies, musicians and artists to cultural organizations, and ministers to churches.

McClelland's classic study showed we have the three needs of power, affiliation, and achievement. Business leaders will tend to have a greater need for power and achievement, politicians and military leaders a greater need for power, and voluntary enterprise leaders a greater need for affiliation.

Two studies conducted by Rawls, Ullrich, and Nelson[94] revealed that profit sector managers placed more value on wealth and security than did those in not-for-profit organizations. Managers in the latter organizations showed greater concerns for status, personal relations, and social recognition. Many people in the field find that not-for-profit personnel have less recognition of the need for aggressiveness in order to succeed.

Voluntary enterprises have always emphasized motives and other rewards over money. Many want to do good, to make changes, to create things, and to mold people. The church offers opportunities to serve God; social service organizations, the opportunity to serve man; education, the joy of study; the arts, self-expression—and all of them offer the opportunity for association with those of like mind. They offer a broad range of motivations for doing things as part of a group—above and beyond the "economic man" concept. The interaction and exchange among the individuals involved can be an end in itself. According to Hicks and Gullet, it

> is perhaps just an exchange of freely expressed thoughts and reactions. This is seen by most persons as rewarding in itself; what one gets as social utilities from other participants is additional gratification. Transcendental organizations including transcendental social exchange, require highly mature participants; not all persons are so mature.[95]

The characteristic lack of measurability in voluntary enterprises may attract and hold persons who are more comfortable in that environment than in business. Those individuals are apt to be less responsive to immediate accountability and numerical measurements, and to have a tolerance for ambiguity. They may also be "softer," less exacting individuals, who do not want to be held accountable to others for performance.

A business is often likened to a predictable machine, while voluntary enterprises tend to conform to an organic model. As Knowles tells us:

> The mechanistic model represents the universe as a machine composed of discrete pieces operating in a spatio-temporal field. These pieces—elementary particles in motion—and their relations form the basic reality to which all other more complex phenomena are ultimately reducible. When forces are applied in the operation of the machine a chain-like sequence of events results; and, since these forces are the only immediate efficient or immediate causes of the events, complete prediction is possible—in principle.[96]

This may account for the relatively greater number of nonconforming "free spirits" you find in the voluntary sector. There is great opportunity (and often need) for flexibility, innovation, and creativity. Many provide an arena for new thought and for molding public opinion. It is an arena in which there are many speeches and publications, where individuals are as often labeled by their beliefs as by their deeds. If business is an environment of numbers, then voluntary enterprise is an environment of words—words concerning beliefs, ideals, and appeals. It is also an environment in which the ego is better fed than the bank account, and honor and recognition for supporters take the place of bonuses and stock options.

Perhaps the more subjective evaluation of success and the lack of the profit motive contribute to the public's high expectations. The public expects a higher degree of fairness, honesty, and accountability from this sector. To the degree that they claim to produce societal good, the groups are under the close scrutiny of society. This puts a great deal of social and moral pressure on the organizations and their people. For example, look at the public indignation at the Brilab and Abscam scandals, or the allegations of misconduct by Cardinal Cody of Chicago. The public reacts less strongly to business misconduct, such as General Electric's price-fixing conviction.

The fact that the principal tool of not-for-profit organizations is voluntarism influences style. On one hand, business emphasizes task-oriented behavior. On the other hand, not-for-profit organizations (with their need to cultivate volunteers and voluntary contributors) emphasize relationship-oriented behavior. Amiability, inoffensiveness, persuasiveness, and a cooperative spirit are highly prized. Max Wortman observed, "Managers work for voluntary organizations because of the possibility of close personal relationships, and close personal relationships tend to be the glue that holds such voluntary organizations together."[97]

The political climate of voluntary enterprises attracts persons who respond to such a milieu. There is often an emphasis on perception over actuality, and on the need to attract a following. Personality, popularity, and the ability to inspire and generate enthusiasm are much-sought-after attributes.

Multiple purposes add to the environment of subjectivity and ambiguity. Persons with a need for clear-cut goals, measurable objectives, and unity of purpose will not be comfortable in enterprises with multiple goals—particularly if the goals change often and the priorities are unclear. The general complexity found in the not-for-profit sector can lack focus and order. It often attracts people who enjoy juggling many things at once or who have a holistic way of thinking that relates well to complexity. You have to find satisfaction "in the doing," for it is hard to know precisely where you stand in terms of tangible accomplishment. If you are part of the service-providing system, it is relatively easy to accept resources as "given" and unrelated to what you do or how well you do it.

Professionals such as educators, social workers, and clergy predominate in not-for-profit organizations. They are present in much greater relative numbers than in most businesses, and they are usually the important people. Among many professionals, the title "manager," or more often "administrator," is used in a condescending way—as sort of an unavoidable function. In voluntary enterprises the professionals are usually "line," while in profit-seeking enterprises they are more often "staff." (In this, business firms dominated by professionals, such as research organizations, have much in common with voluntary enterprises.) Professionals usually have a primary loyalty outside of the organization that pays their salary. They might be marching to one drummer while the organization has a different beat. They are strongly attuned to the expectations, values, and mores of their profession. They often get their rewards from the satisfaction of their profession, and think of themselves as individual practitioners rather than as "organizational" people.

Etzioni cites two studies concerning professionals as follows:

Gouldner (1957) in a study of university professors: "The expert's skills are continually being refined and developed by professional peers outside of his employing organization. Moreover, his continued standing as a competent professional often cannot be validated by members of his own organization, since they are not knowledgeable enough about it. For these reasons, the expert is more likely than others to esteem the good opinion of professional peers elsewhere; he is disposed to seek recognition and acceptance from 'outsiders'. We can say that he is more likely to be oriented to a reference group composed of others not a part of his employing organization, that is, an 'outer reference group'." Wilensky (1956) found the same professional, "outer," reference group among some of the types of experts he studied in labor unions. "The Professional Service expert is oriented in his job role toward an outside colleague group; his primary job identification is with his profession."[98]

In addition to professionals, other types of knowledge workers make up a high proportion of not-for-profit personnel. Knowledge work is more intangible than physical work. It is not as precise in measurement or sequence as manual work and must, by its nature, be designed by the worker himself. The output of knowledge workers (and professionals) is more subject to the influence of morale, mood, human relations, and character than that of manual workers.

Aspects of Social Character

I have touched on factors that help shape voluntary enterprise social character because of the types of individuals they attract. But an organization is more than a collection of people. It develops a character and style of its own.

If an organization is well known as having a distinctive social character and style of operation, that style will tend to become exaggerated. "Our kind of people," therefore, becomes polarized from "those others." As time passes, a particular type of personality will be drawn to one organization rather than to another. The organization increasingly will tend to employ persons who are similar to those it already has. Enterprises that place a premium on good human relations are especially prone to do so. It makes the work force more compatible, more cohesive, and less likely to develop conflicts. Values are especially important to not-for-profit organizations, so persons from the outside who have the same values as those on the inside are likely candidates. As time passes, tradition makes its contribution. Behaviors become entrenched. It is a process of institutionalization that sets an existing style in concrete.

Organizational leadership should consider a variety of aspects of their organizational image and style. Social character being what it is, it is difficult to isolate some aspects as positive and others as negative. They simply *are*. You will gain by understanding them and building your management approach on their realities.

It is well established that many persons employed by voluntary enterprises have their primary loyalties outside the organizational boundaries. These include cause-oriented, dedicated persons, professionals, "craftsmen," and many other knowledge workers. In terms of persons with this "other loyalty," let me deal first with the dedicated personality.

Highly dedicated individuals in both the volunteer corps and the staff are a mixed blessing. The more cause-oriented an enterprise, the more likely will be a large proportion of this kind of personnel. The fires in their boiler room were lighted by their cause, and they generate energy that can be available to the organization. To them the cause is everything. The organization is just so much machinery, if probably necessary. Should the organization shift its course, their course will not shift. Inside or outside, under this banner or another, nothing really matters but their personal commitment and relation to the cause. They have much heat, and sometimes light. They have much energy, and sometimes ability. You have no problem keeping them motivated, but plenty keeping them in harness. Whether the cause be God, country, art, the ERA, or saving whales, the dedicated person has a potent plus to offer—as long as what he has to contribute can be aligned with organizational goals.

Professionals might or might not be quite as dedicated to "the cause." But they do tend to have a loyalty to their profession, their calling, or their work that transcends the organization itself. From the perspective of a leader whose loyalty is to the enterprise itself, the professional can be a potent ally or a thorn in the flesh. Under any condition, his independent spirit and his education give him power. If the organization hosts many of the same type, they can well set its personality and value system. The professionals and the administrators could be two distinct power blocks. Trying to change course if the professionals are not in accord is like trying to change the orientation of a gyroscope. Be they curators, ministers, physicians, educators, social workers, or musicians, they will have an affinity for each other, and will tend to react in concord.

Often the managers began as professionals and were promoted (or demoted) to administrative functions. They can be sensitive to the needs and attitudes of other professionals, and they may be accepted as part of the fraternity. But they are rarely trained in management, and they often maintain their professional orientation toward management and managers. The pros and cons of the manager-professionals were hotly debated in the 1970s over whether the curator should be the top administrator at New York's Metropolitan Museum of Art.

Professionals, traditionally, are not subject to an evaluation based on performance. They are not especially concerned about concepts of efficiency, productivity, performance standards, or quantitative objectives. Their tradition has been one of self-evaluation and ethical standards policed by the profession—not by an employer. The older or more advanced the profession, the less able the lay public is to evaluate its work. They have taken advantage of this circumstance, affiliated with each other, set standards, and generally sought to make entry into the profession more and more difficult for the outsider. Seeing the status attached to professions and their other advantages, almost every occupational group is now in the process of trying to modify itself into a profession.

Within the organization that utilizes many professionals, the need is for the professional to perform a finite function. In a management sense, the leaders of the enterprise are trying to plug the individual into the organization to reach certain objectives—not to enhance professional status or provide an environment for the self-actualization of the professional himself. (This may be a very worthwhile means, but unless the organization is designed to serve the profession, it will have some other end as its reason for existence.) Given the chance, a professional person could move into a negative internalized posture and cease to be effective in his organizational function. The academician could engage in learning as a personally satisfying input and neglect passing it on in useful research or in educating students. The attorney could get so involved in an interesting point of law that the client is not well served. A physician could become more interested in the disease than in the welfare of the patient. A social worker could become more preoccupied with the living sociology about him than in helping people with their plight. A pastor could spend his time studying theology in the abstract to the neglect of the sheep who look to him as shepherd. The manager's job is to achieve certain objectives, utilizing the time and talents of such professionals.

Writing in the *Harvard Business Review*, Cecily C. Selby says that in organizations with influential professionals, "One can usually find two or three management hierarchies: administrative and/or professional and/or voluntary."[99] She goes on to note:

> The professionals may be grouped into professional hierarchies or sub-organizations and committees whose accountabilities are not directly or solely to the board or to the public and the consumers of service. Examples are academic councils, private and state medical and legal accreditation associations, state education authorities, and associations of university professors. There is also the allegiance of the artist and the intellectual to his own sense of creative integrity—an accountability that can override all others.

Michael Maccoby, in his excellent study reported in *The Gamesman*, describes types of executives with their own styles.[100] One is the "craftsman." He respects the work ethic and has a concern for thrift, quality, and people. His interest is not in acquiring riches or power, or for glory and fame. He does not particularly get excited about organizational prestige, growth, or success. "When he talks about his work," writes Maccoby, "his interest is in the process of making something. He enjoys building. He sees others, co-workers as well as superiors, in terms of whether they help or hinder him in doing a craftsman-like job." There are many craftsmen working with people in voluntary enterprises. They work for many of the same reasons volunteers volunteer, except they do it full time and get paid for it. Many are professionals; many are not.

The emphasis on human relations creates a collegial environment. The study by Rawls, Ullrich, and Nelson[101] showed that not-for-profit managers are more concerned with personal relations than are profit sector managers. When dealing with volunteers, subordinates, and supervisors, they tend to be participative and collegial in style. The shared values and information, the seeking of consensus, the nonroutine tasks, the openness, and the imprecise measurements all reinforce the collegial atmosphere. This style affects objectives: When choices are made between task values and humanistic values, the latter often prevail. In this organizational environment, executives are often promoted for reasons other than their management ability. They neither perceive of themselves as managers nor behave in a typical "managerial" style. Many avoid hard data, quantitative measures, and objective evaluation. When faced with choices, they avoid immediate realities rather than deflate a spirit of hope and optimism. The incentives and rewards are more often based on attitude and human relations than on tangible progress.

A study by Robert Gatewood and James Lahiff[102] found that relations with colleagues was ranked higher by managers in voluntary enterprises than by business managers. They concluded that this was to be expected because not-for-profit managers have few other tools "to influence worker behavior other than the personal relationships he establishes with them." They also noted that this ranking increased in organizations in which volunteers played a major role. The presence of volunteers in the organizations contributes to the collegial environment with its emphasis on humanistic values.

Style also feels the impact of the organizations' involvement with the community. Organizational purpose, greater public scrutiny, the influence of a constituency, dependence on the community for financial support, political constraints, and the presence of volunteers within the organization structure—all make their contribution to style. The Gatewood and Lahiff study confirms this.[103] Voluntary enterprise managers studied rated community involvement higher than did the business managers. Organizations that depended on volunteers rated community involvement as being significantly more important to them than did other not-for-profit organizations. As a part of open organizations, voluntary enterprise managers are more dependent on community involvement, and successful organizations reflect this in their style.

Style is also affected by the relatively higher educational level found among staffs of voluntary enterprises. It is routine for executives to hold graduate degrees in their specialty. In many cases a graduate degree is mandatory at the entry level.

This often draws a clear line dividing the staff, with the chiefs on one side and the Indians on the other. Lower-echelon employees may face a barrier, based upon their ability and experience, preventing their upward migration. Horatio Alger stories of starting in the mail room or on the assembly line and ending up as president of the company rarely apply. You do not start out as an orderly and become a neurosurgeon without stepping outside for additional schooling. The sexton doesn't work his way up to bishop, the file clerk to full professor, or the bone-duster to curator without an intervening education. This not only restrains upward mobility but also limits lateral mobility. While a personnel manager, salesman, or top manager can move out of one business line into another with relative ease, many who work in voluntary enterprises find themselves locked into a relatively narrow field. As they enter the field it is fairly well accepted that they are making a lifelong commitment. Early withdrawal usually exacts a great penalty.

The better educated a person is, the less likely you are to exact unquestioning obedience from him. He thinks independently and is capable of drawing his own conclusions. He is more malleable but can quickly weary of routine. A less educated person might succeed because he can see his target clearly in black and white, without complicating it with qualifications and conditions. Managers of better educated personnel devote less time to structuring the work and exercising strict control, and more time as a team coordinator and in representing the group to the next level of the hierarchy. There is a wide range of differences based on educational level and a correspondingly wide range of styles.

The complexity of voluntary enterprises contributes to their character and style. The complex social system of a voluntary organization receives a special mix of talents to manage. The managers who manage well, while simultaneously leading the organization toward its objectives, are resourceful, innovative, and skilled in dealing with people. On the negative side, when one is less successful in such complex organizations, there is much buck-passing, timidity, inertia, and preoccupation with the process instead of results. This preoccupation with the process is a combination of attempting to involve all factions and cover all bases in a complex decision-making matrix, while simultaneously protecting the responsible staff persons. In some organizations this preoccupation becomes the major activity—a substitution for results. A complex internal society, as opposed to a straight-line, orderly, profit-motivated climate, definitely influences management style.

Because of the nature of their purposes, their being subject to much public scrutiny, and their dependence on trust to attract contributions and volunteers, voluntary enterprises place a premium on integrity. Honesty, responsibility, conscientiousness, maturity, and a concern for others mix together with their idealism. Goals are often unattainable, and high motives are often valued above goal attainment. Self-sacrifice is held in high esteem. Ethical practices are expected. This places a heavy load of expectations on the shoulders of all executives, especially top management.

Business publications regularly feature articles in which the leader is asked to identify his own management style. He is presented with a list that will include such labels as autocratic, democratic, laissez faire, and charismatic. In voluntary enterprises many can be tagged with the last two labels. The presence of multiple purposes, many professionals and well-educated persons, and an intermixture of volunteers with staff result in the laissez faire style. (Individuals do pretty much as they please.) There is great pressure to choose this mode when your "followers" are strongly independent and you lack leverage in dealing with them. Studies show that this is one of the least effective styles in business. I am not aware of comparable studies of effectiveness in the voluntary sector, but I do know that it is a common style among many successful organizations.

The charismatic style, functioning under a charismatic leader, is quite apparent when not-for-profit and business leaders are compared— in the latter by their scarcity, and in the former by their prevalence. Charisma is almost essential among the founders of voluntary enterprises. Allegiance to a strong and gifted leader is necessary to elicit a following and the funds to get a movement going. Once the momentum overcomes the initial inertia, charisma is not as essential. Nevertheless, the charismatic personality is a valuable asset in attracting the resources and generating the commitment and enthusiasm so important to the voluntary sector.

The difference in the reward systems of the two sectors influences style. The rewards in voluntary enterprises are centainly not financial. Ambition, though present, is not open. Rewards tend to be built around personal goals other than financial ones: fame, recognition, reputation, influence, having one's way, and hearing that one has clout in the community. These are some of the different aspects of the characteristic modes of behavior called style. It is that which is more easily recognized than described. It is what makes groups of bank accountants, car salesmen, geology professors, Episcopal priests, and women's hairdressers noticably different from each other.

Implications for Management

How does an individual mold his management approach in the light of this distinctive style? Can this quality, so difficult to describe, be categorized sufficiently to provide a basis for management generalities? Perhaps not in any precise sense. Perhaps it should suffice to suggest simply that you become sensitive to differences in style, learn to adapt your methodology to the most appropriate style, and discover your own most effective mode. But I will attempt to outline a few generalizations about style that might be helpful.

The relatively heavy weight given to humanistic values over task accomplishment is worthy of attention. The Blake and Mouton "managerial grid" method[104] plots managerial skill in relation to two axes. One measures the individual's orientation in relation to task accomplishments, the other in terms of human relations. Studies done primarily in the profit-seeking sector show that the least effective styles are those that appear on the grid clinging to one side or the other. The more effective styles represent some sort of combination of the two orientations. Dr. Blake told me that no significant studies have been made exclusively with the voluntary sector. But a commonsense assumption would be that the style that would elicit the greatest results with volunteers would be that which leans to the human relations side, while the one that works best with paid staff would lie somewhere between a good volunteer leadership style and a good profit sector style.

Because the voluntary enterprise manager must manage both paid staff and volunteers, he should adapt his style to that most appropriate for each of the two groups. The approach requires a regular shifting of gears. The resultant eclectic style will match the two types of relationships and the approach he applies to the two types of personnel.

Peter Drucker says that the Roman Catholic Church rotates temperaments in the office of a bishop.[105] If one has a pastoral style (strong human relations orientation), his successor will be assigned because of his administrative (task orientation) or theological (scholarly specialty) style. According to Drucker, the church "learned long ago that the three qualifications—those of pastor, theologian, and administrator—are unlikely to be found in one person. Yet all three are needed to keep a diocese alive." Many voluntary enterprises solve the problem with a somewhat dual leadership. It is common to find a charismatic/ entrepreneur type in double harness with a management type. The one inspires, attracts resources, sets the philosophical tone, and stirs up new opportunities. The other keeps the ship on course and applies the resources to the tasks. I have seen this work quite well, and I have also seen it work just about as well as any schizophrenic personality.

The important thing to remember is that the workers make the leader. One style will work best with one kind of worker, and another with another. Soldiers and artists will respond to different styles. Jazz musicians and IRS auditors march to different drummers. Professional tackles and philosophy professors respond differently to direction. So choose the style most appropriate to the style of the people in the organization. If you are not particularly adaptable, then choose carefully the kind of organization most responsive to your kind of style.

Though the mixture of staff and volunteers accounts in part for the emphasis on human relations, it affects style in its own right. If you are not intentional in what you do, paid staff could begin to think of themselves as paid volunteers with a volunteer type of accountability. Taken to the other extreme, a manager could estrange volunteers if he becomes autocratic and attempts to exact accountability from volunteers in a way that oversteps his authority to enforce it.

In enterprises in which paid and volunteer workers are so intermixed that the two classes of individuals are actually part of the same work groups, the two should be supervised toward group objectives and expectations, and not as individuals. I personally believe that for the manager's own purposes, he should have clear-cut written objectives as to what is being done on behalf of volunteers at all levels, and what is to be accomplished by volunteers. With both expressive and instrumental objectives in mind, he can develop a style that takes both into consideration. In voluntary enterprises it is the followers who largely determine how successful the leader is and how much power is vested in him to do what he is paid to do.

The mixing of volunteers and staff in an open system is usually best dealt with by having a lot of small work groups of volunteers, with paid staff responsible for the objectives of each. The organizational design should be flexible, with plenty of cooperation, interaction, and coordination among the groups. The informal communication networks should be utilized to advantage rather than opposed or forced into an artificial formal network. Overlapping destructive competition or conflict should be dealt with through consensus whenever possible. The structure should be organic rather than mechanistic. Remember: A voluntary enterprise is usually very labor-intensive. If greater productivity is to be attained, it will usually be through eliciting more energy through growth in the number of volunteers. Impatience and a hard-line authoritarian style will yield orderly paper work but lowered productivity.

The presence of professionals, dedicated people, and craftsmen needs special attention. All these types of people are strongly influenced by normative forces. The expectations of their colleagues may strongly influence their behavior. Their standing with their peer group may be more important than salary or a promotion to a higher administrative position. These factors reduce their manager's power in providing utilitarian rewards. Indeed, Etzioni suggests that it is more effective for superiors to exercise limited power over such subordinates.[106] If your objective is to reach certain organizational objectives as a cooperative team, how do you do it when people you have to do it with have other objectives? What if the professionals are motivated by a desire for status outside the organization; what if the dedicated persons are motivated by a dramatic ideal but find it hard to relate necessary groundwork to that ideal; and what if everybody is a "craftsman," delighting in his independent job satisfactions with little regard for group goals? I asked myself these questions some 20 years ago when I became chief executive officer of an organization with exactly that problem.

There were other problems too. Our 60 employees were disbursed among 20,000 volunteers in 15 offices on four continents. Most of our work was in remote areas in the Third World, and the dedication and sacrifice attached to it carried a certain mystique. A lot of our personnel were authentic romantic/charismatic personalities in their own right. Our fund-raising and service-producing systems were poorly coordinated, and our charismatic/entrepreneurial founder, whose image held the organization together, was over 80 years old.

I was able to handle these problems, but the greatest problem was in coping with the style of the personnel. I needed to get our objectives aligned, and to make the people more productive in terms of organizational survival. Let me describe the steps I took as a case study of one way of dealing with "other-directed" people.

We had multiple purposes clustered around a system for teaching people to read. Contributors gave money to "teach the world to read." In addition to individual ambitions, parts of the organization were working toward such goals as "liberating" women in Pakistan, using literacy education as an evangelistic tool for missionaries, promoting a new way of spelling the English language, making our teaching methods more acceptable to the academic fraternity, providing community development in rural Latin America, fighting hunger by improving agricultural methods, publishing reading material for the newly literate, teaching people to read in the classroom, and training volunteer tutors to do the actual teaching. Most of the people were trained in the profession. They were extremely dedicated. Each was doing his own thing.

The first thing I did was to enlarge and strengthen the board. I expanded it from 3 family members and an elderly volunteer friend to 16 substantial and successful men and women, many with international reputations in their fields, and 2 whom you would call "famous." This gave us stability by having an authority base in addition to our founder. I then identified our central purpose—"to teach adults to read"—and our two principal methods—"by training literacy workers, and publishing literacy materials." We then identified a quantitative measurement for each of the two methods and developed cost-effectiveness measures of output—how much cost to train one tutor or to publish one booklet. Each geographical unit was required to report monthly on those output figures. Reports were ultimately given to the board. At the end of the first year, each unit set its own goals for the succeeding year. In three years our output had increased by 400%.

I did a lot of other things in those years, but stabilizing and strengthening the source of authority, reducing our goals to measurable essentials, and letting subgroups set their own goals worked wonders. I had to adapt to their style, but their personal agendas began to align with the purposes for which the contributors were giving their money. I then developed a detailed long-range hierarchy of objectives, some 100 pages in length, to take us into the next decade.

I had to tailor my own style to the uniqueness of the situation. I needed a strong board to balance the beloved but impetuous, flamboyant, and vacillating founder. In dealing with the professionals, I knew they would not accept close supervision, and that they must have responsibility and autonomy to set their own goals and manage their own work. Given the geographical dispersion, there was not much choice. All the dedicated personnel needed was a better hierarchy of purposes, which was sanctioned by the founder. The craftsmen were already in accord with the central purpose; the reporting mechanism gave them an incentive, and the central office a means of upgrading their effectiveness. The measure of output and cost-effectiveness allowed us for the first time to manage. There was now supervision and control of the work, albeit very general supervision and relative control.

If you have a strong personality, you need not fear exercising it in a charismatic leadership style. It is a style in which the personality force of the individual elicits and channels human energy through what Etzioni calls "diffuse and intense influence over the normative orientation" of others. Organizations that are identified with causes, that depend on recruiting volunteers and raising funds, that are concerned with expressive "ends" as well as instrumental "means," that have a significant political component, that can potentially attract boundless resources, and that have an appropriate social character can respond well to a charismatic leader. The best places for such leaders are on top or in "line" positions and in jobs requiring a generalist rather than a specialist or segmentalist. Charismatic personalities are more effective in positions where cohesion is essential than in those where cohesion is unimportant. They also function better in jobs where creativity and innovation are more important than routine or maintenance operations. They make a greater contribution in tasks requiring loose control rather than close control, intense involvement rather than low involvement, and in those where inspiration of others is required.

Conclusion

Voluntary enterprises tend to have a distinctive social character and a characteristic management style. Once this style becomes entrenched, it can intensify. The social character is influenced by the kinds of persons who are attracted to the organizations, and by the nature of the work that the organizations do. Idealists, professionals, persons who can tolerate ambiguity, and persons who are specialists in the type of service provided—all contribute to this character. Wealth is less important than status to many of them. They often stress human relations over task accomplishment. Organizational style is often characterized by innovations and flexibility, and there is usually a premium on political, consensus, and human-relations processes.

Managers must learn to lead dedicated persons, professionals, craftsmen, and knowledge workers in general. Dealing with the volunteer contingent requires special skills. Integrity and trust are especially important because of community involvement and the need to motivate and build cohesion among the constituency. A charismatic management style is often successful in the voluntary sector, especially in attracting funds and a following. Rewards and motives of a nonfinancial nature are valuable, especially in dealing with the volunteer corps.

The great weight given to human values in the typical voluntary enterprise indicates that managers would rank high on concern for human relations. They must be adaptable to the various types of followers in the organization, and should be skilled in working with small task-groups.

14

BOUNDLESS RESOURCES

How much would it cost to air a TV commercial narrated by the president of the United States on every station in the nation?

It all depends on what you want to advertise. If the president was a Boy Scout and you want to promote scouting, he will donate his services and the stations will contribute their time. But if you want him to sell razor blades. . . .

The resources available to voluntary enterprises are not as limited as those available to profit-seeking organizations. Since benefits from their success do not accrue to proprietors or stockholders, and since contributions of goods, services, money, and expertise are tax-deductible, nonprofit organizations can draw resources from many areas. Huge quantities of effort and time are given. And voluntary enterprises may share both tangible and intangible resources with each other. Referral of clients, joint ventures, and shared resources are common among such organizations, with no financial exchange whatsoever. For example, a church group borrows trucks each month from Goodwill Industries to transport commodities and distribute them to the poor. The giving away of "trade secrets"—far from being treasonous—is often a symbol of an organization's leadership status. For example, the Shepard's Center, a St. Louis program, pioneered an approach to multipurpose services to senior citizens. With the encouragement and management assistance of its founder, centers based on the St. Louis model were established in other cities. In the profit-seeking sector they would have been fee-paying franchises. In the voluntary sector there was neither fee nor organizational linkage.

The virtually unlimited resource pool that (under the right circumstances) could be tapped exists because of two basic facts: First, no owner benefits financially; second, there are societal goals to be attained. With our value system, we look down on an individual's getting something for nothing. We do not knowingly contribute or freely lend things to businesses. A business should pay for what it gets; costs are a "given" for profits. With the same system of values, we look with favor on responsible organizations' providing services for the common good. In its nonprofit setting, the parents of little leaguers gladly pay for their child's opportunity to play ball. But if someone were to profit from the games, even the players would expect payment.

The voluntary enterprise enacts the role of a broker. It gathers resources and matches them to needs. It provides a conduit for transferring ideas, attitudes, values, and resources from those who have them to those to whom the contributor is willing to give. As long as the organization is perceived to make this transfer without enriching itself, it is thanked. When the enterprise adds value to the resources in the process, it is applauded.

Having such a wealth of resources available is also related to the more open-system nature of many voluntary enterprises. Voluntary enterprises tend to be open systems to a greater degree than do business enterprises. For example, a coal mine is a relatively closed system. There is a finite amount of coal in the location. The mine's boundaries are known and there is little interchange with forces beyond those boundaries. Not-for-profit enterprise boundaries are often unknown, difficult to define, or infinite. Open systems interchange energy (in the form of information and activities) with their social environment. While this may be frustrating to an orderly management mind, it allows the organization readily to incorporate a variety of resources. In contrasting closed and open systems, you might visualize a railroad and a highway system. The railroad is a relatively closed system with precise boundaries. The operators control what goes in one end, and they can predict what comes out at the other. The highway is a more open system, which draws in its traffic and disburses it at many points.

An open system can elicit energy from its surrounding environment. So it does not "run down" with the consumption of a finite resource pool. The input of this energy counteracts the operation of entropy. More like a biological than a mechanical system, it is not as restrained by the cause-and-effect relationships of a closed system.

Aspects of Voluntary Enterprise Resources

This relative abundance of resources is obviously a great advantage for voluntary enterprises.

Tracy Connors, then president of the National Association of Public

Service Organization Executives, pointed out to me that nonprofit organizations have far more options in terms of "combinations of people,
financial resources, strategies, and coalitions to accomplish their goals
than does the typical for-profit organization."[107]

Financial resources can be acquired in many of the same ways as
they are in business. Nonprofit organizations cannot get capital by selling stock, but they can issue interest-bearing bonds. They can borrow
money, and they can invest. They are eligible for certain grants and
contracts that are not available to business enterprises. They can acquire
and operate profit-seeking businesses. They can operate a department
or one of their ancillary services as a business. For example, a hospital
might own a cafeteria, a museum might own a bookstore, or a trade
association might publish a magazine. In addition to such businesslike
tangential operations, they can charge for their services to cover all or
part of their costs. Occasionally, organizations are profit-seeking in
every way except in their legal status and in how they distribute their
surplus. The American Automobile Association and the National Geographic Society are examples.

Contributions of goods and services are common. When equipment
has been fully depreciated by a tax-paying company, it is contributed to
a not-for-profit group. Dow Chemical, for example, might contribute a
copying machine, a typewriter, and filing cases to a counseling center
after the equipment has been fully depreciated on its books. A utility
might contribute an older-model computer to a voluntary enterprise that
feeds hungry people in developing countries. The groups might be eligible to receive free surplus commodities or to buy surplus equipment
from the government. Sea scouts and deep-sea research organizations
solicit contributions of boats. Landlords allow groups to occupy vacant
space on a temporary basis. Perishable commodities are given to a children's home before they spoil on the shelves or in the fields.

Services donated in what would otherwise be "down time" can
benefit both the contributor and the recipient alike. For instance, a com-
merical artist might do the layout for a blood drive between his paid
jobs. In the process, he meets a new group of potential customers and
exposes them to his talents. Architects, attorneys, engineers, and accountants might handle minor matters without charging, and major
ones on a cost-only basis. Though the practice is less common than it
once was, discounts and perquisites might be given to the nonprofit
executives in the form of free or discounted merchandise, club mem-
berships, free passes, and demonstrator automobiles.

A business can ask its employees to work, but it cannot ask others
to do so. A voluntary enterprise can. Contributed energy in the form of

time and effort is a resource peculiar to the voluntary enterprise. Most informal and many small formally constituted organizations operate exclusively by volunteer labor. In others, a tiny cadre of paid persons provide continuity and staff services to hundred of volunteers. Board members, management volunteers, and direct-service workers contribute their time and effort. On occasion a business might loan an executive or some other employee to work for the voluntary enterprise for days or even months. A dramatic example is the American Association of Petroleum Landmen. Whatever company employs the president of the association is expected to give him a year's sabbatical leave with pay to perform his volunteer president's functions. Organizations vary in the degree to which they utilize this asset, but it is a resource not available to the business sector.

Public-service time on radio and television, or free newspaper advertising in the form of announcements and feature stories, is often not appreciated for the valuable asset it is. The corner drugstore will let Junior Achievement or the Young Women's Christian Association put up a poster but would not consider such a display for Sperry-Rand or IBM. A bank will make its branches available as a location where clients can register for a not-for-profit ambulance service. The phone company could insert a flyer in its monthly bills. Access to communications media can be used to publicize events, to recruit volunteers, to raise funds, and to inform and educate. Except for an occasional newsworthy event or unusual new product, business concerns must pay advertising rates for comparable exposure.

Personalities who have accumulated great wealth by public appearances and endorsements for profit-seeking ventures might donate their talents to draw attention to a cause in which they are interested. Sally Struthers raises funds for the Christian Children's Fund, Danny Thomas for St. Jude's Hospital, President Reagan for the Special Olympics, Johnny Cash for programs for prisoners, and Bob Hope for a variety of charities.

Other voluntary enterprises will share their services or enter into joint ventures. This is often done without any exchange of funds. It can often be a win–win situation, in which the clients of the two agencies benefit and each organization reaches its own objectives. For example, the Family Service Society conducts a program at a community center. One organization gets clients with no enlistment costs, while the other gets free services. Cultural groups need audiences, and clubs, churches, and other groups have audiences that welcome exhibits and performances. Without a formal accounting procedure, an organization with vehicles might loan them to an organization that would in turn make its building available. A large corps of volunteers might work a few weeks to help out a sister organization in an emergency. The possibilities of coalitions, exchanges, and cooperative activities are almost unlimited.

But there are negative aspects of limitless resources, a dark lining to even this silver cloud.

When your hand is out, you don't know what will be dropped in it. The adage "Don't look a gift horse in the mouth" often translates, "You can't look a gift horse in the mouth." When the board chairman's wife walks in one morning and announces that she is going to redecorate the executive director's office, it is hard to say no. The donated artwork might clash with your taste. You might have no need for the donated file cabinets. The architect could present you with an ill-designed eyesore. The recipient of a gift does not have the same control as the purchaser.

You should remember the plight of persons in India who were so unfortunate as to be given a white elephant. The poor recipient could not, by custom, either work or kill the beast, and he was expected to provide it with first-class attention and care. A white elephant has come to symbolize gifts with a net negative valve.

Often, unsolicited resources will be offered that appear initially as unencumbered windfalls. However, on closer scrutiny they prove to have strings attached. If the concessions required are not worth the value of the contribution, if it is inappropriate to your purposes, or if it would generate burdensome additional costs, the gift may have to be refused. You can protect yourself from such problems by having the foresight to set policies and procedures regarding such matters. Policies prevent personnel from getting emotionally involved in dealing with potential contributors of undesirable goods or services.

Occasionally, the opportunity to come into a wealth of resources may tempt the enterprise to divert its course. Faced with such an opportunity, the paid management might want to accept it, and the board to refuse. For example, a technical assistance program set up to help the farmers of southern India might be offered massive support to perform the same service for Sri Lanka. A community center that concentrates on helping disadvantaged youth could get double funds if they switched to senior adults.

Alan Andreason of the University of Illinois[108] gave me an example of the challenge this is to museums: "Many have expanded their revenue rather substantially by getting into the business of marketing reproductions, artifacts, postcards, and paintings. In many cases their little boutiques generate more than half of their revenue." While this can be an asset to the institution and its principal objectives, it can also create tensions. Dr. Andreason added: "Many who lend their support see expansion in this direction as a bit tarnishing to the organization. There is often among the charter members of any organization the feeling that it should remain pure and true." Forecasting and other aspects of planning can be difficult when the receipt of a generous influx of resources might come unexpectedly. True, this is a good kind of problem to have, but it could confuse the sense of order and give the staff a feeling of uncertainty.

Volunteer workers can be "turned off" just as easily as they can be "turned on." An open door can be used to go in or out. Volunteers can exit at a crucial time, just as they can enter when they are most needed. Management has neither the short-term nor the long-term control over (volunteer) personnel that business has.

The open-organization nature of voluntary enterprises makes the inflow of resources possible. While its positive attributes are many, there is also a negative side. Relative outsiders mix and mingle physically with staff members in their offices. Privacy is rare and confidentiality difficult. Volunteers get involved in staff tensions, personality clashes, and power struggles. Entry-level staff members could seek to handle grievances through influential volunteers not sensitive to the chain of command. Volunteers who provide assistance on one project could assume authority not theirs for giving assignments to staff. Employees easily become confused when they receive conflicting directions. The collegial nature of the open organization has many subtle undertones that could be violated by the uninitiated.

The wealth of resources available to voluntary enterprises is by far one of their major advantages. But management must be alert to many possible negative aspects.

Resource Management

Not-for-profit enterprises that have the opportunity to tap such a variety of resources would want to limit themselves solely to business processes. Businesses do not have the opportunity to plan and organize their operations with the prospect of such resources in mind.

The identification, development, and solicitation of resources is a function with no exact parallel in business. Therefore, a systematic method for handling these activities must be established. A business goes to various markets and exchanges resources it has for resources it requires; a voluntary enterprise often gives nothing for what it receives. It can be argued that the giver receives satisfaction, a sense of accomplishment, or recognition for what he gives. Yet the receiving entity is not diminished. With this potential for resources, an organization should plan, establish appropriate systems, assign specific objectives to responsible individuals, and carry out activities specifically designed to exploit opportunities within its reach.

Peter Spurney, whose professional expertise lies in planning and implementing major public events such as World's Fairs and Olympic Games, has developed his own approach for tapping and managing the in-kind resources available to such major undertakings. When I worked with him on the 1984 Louisiana World Exposition in New Orleans, he shared with me some of his procedures.[109] At the outset, he costs everything out and prepares a list of potential resources that might be contributed to offset the items in the budget. The resources might include advertising, physical objects, volunteer time, or donated services. Because of the glamour of the events on which he has worked, he notes, "I have always been able to give a little in return for some of these contributions. For example, designating the donor as the 'official Olympics airline,' or the 'official' soft drink of a World's Fair."

Spurney endorses the idea of getting together a group of knowledgeable people to focus on the need for contributed resources and "brainstorm" ideas. "You come up with all sorts of wild and imaginative schemes . . . you stimulate their thinking and develop an environment of creativity, flexibility, and innovation where people say, 'The whole world is out there. What do they have that we need?'"

The development of an awareness of the almost unlimited resources available is an asset to any organization. Like Peter Spurney, you might even assign a staff person with the responsibility of identifying and developing such resources. Management should encourage alertness to potential resources among all those connected with the enterprise. You never know who might find an opportunity. I remember when an organization needed funds to print booklets that had been written in Medellin, Colombia. A volunteer in Wisconsin, whose activities had nothing whatsoever to do with the program in South America, learned of the need through a routine newsletter. She knew that a local paper mill was discontinuing a certain type of paper. Rolls of paper that sold for $70,000 wholesale were donated. They were shipped to Medellin. It was not the proper paper for the books, but the local office traded it to the printer not only for the proper paper but for his printing service as well. Without the cultivation of an atmosphere of alertness to needs, the opportunity would not have been exploited.

A kind of free-wheeling innovating personality can be a valuable asset to a voluntary enterprise. A creative individual, a department, or, for that matter, an entire organization with an open and inventive attitude can generate the original thinking needed to grasp the kinds of opportunities that voluntary enterprises have. Since many of the unique opportunities come in unexpected and unstructured ways, there needs to be a special kind of unstructured ingenuity and receptiveness to recognize and grasp the opportunities.

The organization and its leadership should be more adaptable than rigid in order to accommodate resource opportunities. It should be sufficiently flexible to modify its plans when unexpected and unplanned opportunities appear. Each major opportunity should be evaluated in light of its potential contribution to the ultimate organizational purpose even though it might upset the applecart and send everyone scurrying about in the short term.

Let me give you another example from publishing in Latin America. A program to publish 10,000 booklets was in place for Mexico. The writers had done their work. A relatively large sum had been spent on design, artwork, and layout. The organization was in the final stages of arranging for distribution of the booklets through a Mexican government teaching program. Then came a bombshell that could annihilate all this work and delay the implementation of the plan by a full year. The bombshell was in the form of an unprecedented opportunity. The Spanish-language edition of the *Reader's Digest* was willing to include a similar booklet in every issue—at no cost to the organization.

This opportunity brought disappointment to those who had done so much work on the edition of 10,000. There would be an expensive delay in their program. But the opportunity was overwhelming: a 70-page insert in full color to 400,000 homes! The organization fortunately was flexible enough to accept this amazing input of resources in spite of the fact that it meant a short-term out-of-pocket financial loss.

Conclusion

The quantity of resources available to voluntary enterprises is not as limited as those available to profit-seeking enterprises. The latter must engage in exchange for its inputs, while this is not necessarily the case with the former. This phenomenon exists because no owner makes a profit from voluntarily donated inputs while a societal good can be attained. The voluntary enterprise operates in the role of a broker. It is an open system linking those who have and can be persuaded to give and those who need and are willing to receive.

This resource availability is of great advantage to these organizations. Among the available resources are money, goods, services, time, free advertising, public endorsement by celebrities, and joint ventures with other not-for-profit groups.

There are a few concomitant negative factors. For instance, the voluntary organization has limited control over the nature and quality of what it receives, the organizational purpose could be distorted by resource opportunities, management is more complex, and there can be an outflow as well as an influx of certain resources.

The availability of many resources has management implications. A system for identifying, developing, and soliciting resources is necessary. The organization should be designed to be flexible and alert to opportunity, and willing to alter plans to exploit selected opportunities.

15

STAGGERING CONSUMPTION

A voluntary enterprise can be a burden rather than a contributor to society by consuming more than it produces. It can consume more than it produces and stay alive indefinitely. A business cannot do that.

The comparison is somewhat fallacious, of course. But it provides a good working hypothesis to deal with a problem voluntary enterprises face that is foreign to business. *Voluntary enterprises can persist even though their consumption of resources consistently exceeds their tangible output.*

A business, on the other hand, will cease to exist if it consistently consumes more than it produces. Its purpose is profit. Profit is returned to investors; profit fuels the organizational efforts to produce more goods or services. During its beginning years, a business often consumes more than it produces. It then passes a break-even point, begins to provide a return on investment, and persists as long as it continues to have an output greater than the sum of its inputs. There could be times when it will show a loss. It might be a deliberate tactical short-term loss in a competitive market entered for a potential long-range benefit. It could be due to bad management, or an unfavorable market. But it must be temporary. The enterprise must persist, weather the storm without depleting its resources, and emerge as profitable as ever, or die.

There are subsidized businesses that appear to be independent entities but that are quasi businesses for some illegal or unethical purpose or for a perfectly innocent societal good. For example, a developing nation might set up an airline as a business. It consistently operates at a loss, and continues to have its deficit covered by the national treasury. It is, in fact, not really a profit-seeking enterprise. Its purpose could be to feed the ego of the nation's oligarchy or its president, or it might be a government tool to assist in the industrial or economic development of the nation—promoting tourism, for example. Such businesses are actually part of the government sector, not truly profit-seeking enterprises at all.

But let us return to the voluntary enterprise—a true part of the voluntary sector—an organization whose charter and literature say that it exists to meet some need other than profit, and for which contributions of time and money are voluntarily given. It is possible for such an organization to operate, year in and year out, consuming more money and volunteer time in its operations than it produces in the value of its services. To illustrate, let me pose some actual examples.

1. A center is established in a ghetto to train young men so they can get better jobs. The total of the organization's budget, not counting contributed talent, is greater than the wages of the trained youth.
2. A wartime drive to collect old aluminum pots and pans to overcome the aluminum shortage in the manufacture of airplanes produces scrap aluminum at a cost that greatly exceeds the cost of a conventional aluminum recovery process.
3. A program to train volunteers to teach adults to read in a developing Asian nation costs twice as much per pupil taught than if paid teachers were utilized.
4. A neighborhood project to provide a service for transporting elderly persons to a shopping center costs significantly more per trip, without considering the value of the volunteers' time or gasoline, than if taxi fare were given directly to each client.
5. An organization is formed and an art gallery renovated and operated to sell the work of a group of amateur painters. Annual net sales are consistently less than the participants' costs.
6. A small mission church is established in the inner city by a large, wealthy congregation as an outpost for the express purpose of "bringing lost people to Christ." Five years later, the congregation is very pleased with the mission while the little church in the inner city is preoccupied with the nurture of its members and is producing no converts at all.
7. An annual charity ball costs $40,000. It nets approximately $3000 each year for the charitable cause.
8. Seven sculptors are given a grant to teach the operators of a group of senior-adult centers how to help the old folks enjoy sculpting. Everyone seems pleased with the result, and the grant is renewed. Later, the seniors say they enjoy TV more than sculpting.
9. A small voluntary enterprise has activated itself annually for almost 20 years. My wife is the founder, creative technician, and chief executive. I am its single volunteer. The purpose is to construct six fruitcakes for Thanksgiving and Christmas. Exclusive

of her enthusiastic—and my coerced—labor, each cake costs $12.30. Last year the kids owned up to the fact that they didn't particularly like the cakes. We are at it again right now.

How can this be? It can be because voluntary enterprises are open systems, drawing resources from their environments, and those who benefit from the services are usually not the same as those who provide the resources. What is contributed is not in direct response to value received. The contributor of resources does not necessarily know what value is ultimately transmitted to the client. The recipient does not necessarily know the cost of what he receives.

Therefore, it could be possible for the $40,000 charity ball to go on for a decade, producing its $3,000 each year to help support the neighborhood transportation program, at a total expense of $26.60 for each ride, which could be purchased in a taxi for $11.50. Both the contributors and the clients are happily unaware of their costly exercise.

But the reason this characteristic is often a fallacy is that many organizations have an expressive purpose in addition to their instrumental purpose. And they do not officially acknowledge this purpose. In some cases they are simply not overtly aware of it. The paradox is that some of the inputs are also outputs. The utility or benefit received by contributors, volunteers, and constituency, as a result of providing the inputs, makes this possible. The contributor is relieved of guilt, fulfills a sense of obligation, responds to pressure, seeks to avoid embarrassment, or feels good in the act of giving. The volunteer enjoys the activity itself, or is gaining exposure or experience that is a personal benefit in and of itself. A member may simply enjoy the security or prestige of belonging. As long as they are not confronted with the reality that their outputs are less than their cost, they are content to continue.

So you find that things are not so expensive or absurd as they seem. My wife's fruitcakes bring her more pleasure in the making than the total $75 would buy in books or concerts. The real purpose of the grant for teaching sculpture to senior adults was to provide money for the artists. They didn't put on the charity ball just for the $3,000, but for the fun of it and the social prestige of being on the committee. The national drive to collect aluminum pots and pans was designed at the outset to increase morale and give the citizens a sense of participation in the war effort. So the enterprises did consume more inputs than their stated purpose of outputs. The fallacy lies in that the stated purposes and the *ad hoc* purposes were not the same.

That is not to say that this is always the case. Enterprises, honest and diligent otherwise, have drifted sometimes into an ineffective and nonproductive mode. This would not happen in business. Not because business managers are smarter or more ethical, not because businesses do not drift into postures without recognizing it, but because the resources of a business would dry up. It would be bankrupt. It would not survive.

Aspects of Resource Consumption

The whole idea behind organized effort is *positive synergism*, when two plus two equals more than four, when outputs are greater than the sum of inputs. When *negative synergism* exists—when two plus two equals three, when outputs are less than inputs—the organization is counterproductive. Organizational leaders should be sensitive to the fact that negative synergism can exist in a voluntary enterprise. Forewarned is forearmed. Though it is rare in a total enterprise with paid staff, it is relatively common in the nooks and crannies of organizational life—a project here, a committee there, or a task group in another place.

In considering the facets of this characteristic of voluntary enterprises, let me begin with more on the expressive value of not-for-profit organizations. They are mediums for self-expression. They are organisms in which individuals can find satisfaction and have fun doing things with a group of people with the same interests. If you enjoy children but have none of your own, you can work with Camp Fire Girls or Cub Scouts. If you like pomp and circumstance, join the Shriners or parade with a Mardi Gras krewe. If you like books, volunteer at the library; art, at the museum; baseball, with the Little League; teaching, at a Sunday school class; dancing, at a dancing club. Or if you simply enjoy helping people—take your choice. Getting there is half the fun. Means are as important as ends. The intrinsic rewards in themselves are part and parcel of the instrumental activities. You wish to continue doing them even when there is no rejuvenating payoffs at the end of a work cycle.

We are not here on earth as workmen to manufacture goods or perform services. Work is necessary to meet many of our needs. It can become an end in itself if it is enjoyable or rewarding. But in no way are we here to serve businesses, governments, or any other organization. Mankind was not made for organizations, but organizations for mankind. We love and hate, laugh and play and work, cry, create, and destroy, rise up and lie down. Life is complex and consists of many kinds and levels of experience. We fish, hunt, sail, and build as labor in order to make a living. Or we can do something else for a living, and fish, hunt, sail, and build for fun. There is nothing wrong in expressive activity or in organizations that provide opportunities for such.

Voluntary functions performed as expressive activities are okay. No, they are great.

Expressive purposes in themselves are not the problem. If you do something gratis for others and enjoy it yourself, so much better. If an organization facilitates your need for self-esteem or recognition and helps you feel strong, potent, capable, needed, and useful, it is doing good. If it extends your personality, gives you flexibility and a wide range of choices, or provides a place and means for working off your energy, it is providing a service. If it meets your affiliation needs and brings you together with a compatible group with which you can socialize while working together, it is a beneficial enterprise. If you like to be a leader and the organization gives you a group to lead and a lot of satisfying procedures for your group to undertake, that is good.

The problem lies not with expressive activity itself, for it is a legitimate organizational function. The problem lies in waste or deception. Waste, for example, can grow out of the attitude that since a volunteer is working on behalf of others, anything and everything he does is good. Sincerity and worthy motives are sufficient in themselves. This prevalent attitude does not take the desires or the needs of the recipients into consideration. Neither does it take into consideration the stewardship of energy—the responsibility for accomplishment. The irrelevant discharge of activity is waste. Deception occurs when, through design or ineptness, funds are solicited for a purpose but spent in activity that does not accomplish the purpose. An extreme example is a fund-raising campaign that costs more in dollars and human energy than it brings in.

Another counterproductive circumstance is the creation of dependency. The individual volunteer, group, or entire organization has a desire to do something. They become determined to help someone, whether he needs help or not. Their need to help is so great that they unconsciously make their client dependent upon their efforts to the extent that the client is not encouraged to use his own resources to help himself. The needs of the helper are met. Actually, the roles are reversed, and the client nourishes the "helper" more than the client truly benefits himself.

The federal government's relation to the Cherokee Indians is an excellent example of the effects of dependency. Before the government took control of Cherokee affairs in the late 1800s, the Cherokees had "an educational system which produced a Cherokee population 90 percent literate in its native language and used bilingual materials to such an extent that Oklahoma Cherokees had a higher English literacy level than the white populations of either Texas or Arkansas." In 1969 "the median number of school years completed by the adult Cherokee population is only 5.5; 40 percent of adult Cherokees are functionally illiterate; Cherokee dropout rates in public schools is as high as 75 percent; and the level of Cherokee education is well below the average for rural and nonwhites in the State."[110]

Individuals within an organizational context could pursue only their personal objectives without simultaneously contributing to those of the organization. They could simply use the organism of the enterprise for their own purposes. If enough individuals do this, the output will dissipate until it is less than its inputs. The organism might not die, but as far as the clients are concerned, it might as well be buried.

Implications for Management

An overconsumption of resources is the antithesis of good management. Good management will obviously counter any tendency in this direction and will keep your organization from consuming more than it produces. But additional specific management processes can also be introduced to provide preventive or corrective action.

Periodically, an organization should evaluate its current posture in relation to its reason for being. This evaluating activity should certainly accompany the outset of a new management cycle, as in the undertaking of a new program, an annual reevaluation of its long-range plan, or when new officers assume office. It might be the subject of an executive committee retreat or an annual meeting. One such evaluation might consist of a discussion based on whether the characteristic discussed in this chapter is manifest in your enterprise or any of its components.

Recognize that the potential for intolerable resource consumption should be considered in problem analysis, decision making at various levels, and the activities of the enterprise involving the identification of resources and the exploitation of opportunities. Since organizations do not plan to become victims of negative synergism, it is obvious that they move into it through myriad decisions and actions. A review of how an organization can drift into such a posture over its lifetime should alert you to its dangers.

My friend Arleon Kelley has done some good work on the organizational growth cycle. He diagrams the life of an organization as shown in Figure 2.

The cycle steps include a first phase (1) when people get together

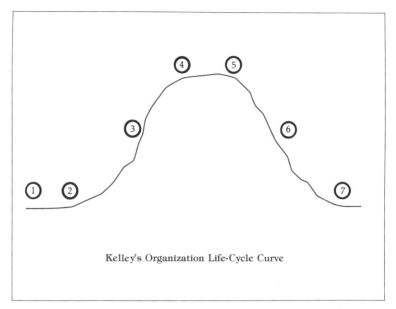

Figure 2. (From *Your Church: A Dynamic Community* by Arleon L. Kelley. Philadelphia: Westminster Press, 1982. Copyright 1982 by Westminster Press. Adapted by permission.)

because they sense a common need. They begin to dream and fantasize the great things they might do together. And out of those common fantasies, they begin to share their energies. This initial step in the ascendancy phase leads to a second step (2) in the organization's life. It is a time when the enterprise undergoes slow growth. The public at large is standing back to see if the enterprise will succeed, whether it will meet some real public need. It is a time when dreams are being translated into specific concrete salable actions, and have an impact on the public. This, in turn, leads to a next step (3) when the organization begins to demonstrate real life. It is a time when they can prove they can really affect the public. It is a time when the public begins to accept it. It is a time when the dreams are being translated into specific and actualized goals. This, in turn, leads to the next step (4) in the organization's life cycle. After a period of rapid growth, an organization tends to enter into a golden mean or plateau. It is effective and mature, continuing to meet the needs of members and communities in the niche it has carved out for itself. Its goals and the needs of the people are in line with each other. It is a time of a sense of well-being. Not unlike, perhaps, the Chinese state of Yen, a state of all is well. Eventually, however, an organization will begin to move into a fifth stage (5). Here the tendency is to become so comfortable that it tends not to make the adjustments required for continued viability. When this happens, it begins to decline. This, in turn, leads to another stage (6) when the decline becomes ever more intense and the enterprise is unable to reshape its goals and get back in touch with the needs of the people. When this occurs, deviation begins to become very evident. People begin to drift out of the organization. Finally, it begins to move into a final stage (7) when it is increasingly preoccupied with its own internal life. When this happens, eventually it crystallizes and dies. But if its supply of resources is replenished, its actual demise will be protracted.

A key factor in keeping an organization viable lies in the preparation of objectives. If the enterprise has both expressive and instrumental purposes, the expressive objectives should be officially recognized and incorporated into the objective-writing process. This will solve a lot of problems. It will improve organizational integrity and give management a handle with which to deal with expressive activities. Though we usually think of objectives as being "bigger and better" in a healthy organization, there is no reason expressive objectives are comparable to cost-cutting. But as long as expressive purposes (that are actually present) are ignored in official objectives, you have little control over them. They are a hidden agenda at every meeting, and the incomplete formal objectives are taken with a grain of salt.

The board and policy-setting process should consciously consider expressive objectives and negative synergism if there is a potential problem. Because of the harm that a tendency in that direction can bring, it is certainly worthy of policy action.

In selecting both paid and volunteer leadership, those who will feed this problem should be screened out altogether, or certainly moved out of key positions. As personnel are oriented, inspired, and indoctrinated in the organization's purposes and traditions, their attention should be focused on productive instrumental achievement.

There should be a plan for phasing negative characteristics out of and positive characteristics into organizational activities. As volunteers are monitored, guided, or supervised, the focus must be on achieving realistic objectives on behalf of the cause or the clients of the enterprise. Awareness of cost-effectiveness should include some measure of the value of volunteer time and effort. Efficient and effective use of time should be stressed.

In the control function, management should be certain that they measure progress toward objectives in terms of the utilization of all resources. Accounting procedures developed in the profit-seeking sector are rightly based on dollars and cents. In the voluntary sector, accounting and other feedback controls should consider the consumption of energy provided by volunteers at all levels, in-kind contributions, and even the contribution of other entities involved in coalitions and joint ventures with your enterprise. You might find that you are being "carried" by some other group to a greater extent than you recognize.

When an enterprise begins to become aware of negative synergism, it sets up a psychological reaction among its leaders. They become defensive, start rationalizing, and look for any evidence to avoid facing reality. Scapegoats are sought. Faced with the fact that a big part of their life may have been spent in *make work*, they feel resentment or despair. Be prepared for such a reaction with a positive package of policies and procedures to turn things around and get the enterprise on the right track.

Conclusion

Voluntary enterprises are subject to a paradox. They can operate and survive even though they consume more resources they produce. Their inputs can consistently be greater than their tangible output. If such a condition were to exist for very long in a business enterprise, bankruptcy would soon bring everything to a halt. This paradox is possible because of the expressive needs met by organizations in the not-for-profit sector. People are willing to work and give to satisfy some of their needs, even when their efforts or dollars fail to produce an equitable outcome.

Obviously, such a situation, especially when allowed to persist over time, is counterproductive. It can produce hypocrisy and fraud. At the least, it creates a never-never land of self-deception and wasted energy that would otherwise be quite useful. This is not to say that expressive activity in itself is wrong. But if the activity instead of the accomplishment is the purpose, it should be honestly and openly acknowledged at the outset.

Management can help counteract tendencies in that direction by periodically and formally evaluating its current posture in relation to its organizational purpose. When goals are defined and objectives written, care should be taken to spell out the expressive as well as the instrumental ones. The more precisely the objectives can be quantified and the more diligently results are measured, the better. Over a period of time the leadership should seek to influence the organizational culture so it becomes oriented toward the attainment of results.

16

THE COMPLEXITY OF VOLUNTARY ENTERPRISES

In the *Laocoön Group,* an ancient Greek sculpture that now stands in the Vatican, a father and his two sons are being crushed to death by sea serpents. The work shows about as much emotion as can be carved into marble. The father's body struggles to free itself from the writhing coils of the serpents. Every feature on his tortured face strains in fear, hopelessness, agony, and the recognition that death awaits his sons and himself.

This complex artwork from the Hellenistic period, of struggling men and intertwining serpents, was uncovered by excavations in the early 16th-century Rome. Virgil described Laocoön's plight, when the serpents "seize and bind in mighty folds . . . twice circling his waist, twice winding . . . around his throat . . . he strains his hands to burst the knots . . . lifts to heaven hideous cries, like the bellowing of a wounded bull."[111] The legendary Trojan priest and his sons will forever fight among the crushing death-grip coils of serpents, sent by the gods to slay them.

Laocoön will forever live the life of a voluntary enterprise manager.

Voluntary enterprises are characteristically more complex than their business counterparts. They are indeed complex, writhing, and difficult to manage. Their multiple purposes, dual internal systems, and other factors generate many more variables for the voluntary enterprise manager than for his profit sector counterpart. Typically, a small voluntary enterprise is as organizationally complex as a much larger business or industrial organization. For example, the Saab Automobile Company's engine factory employs over 400 people in four divisions. One builds engine blocks, another produces cylinder heads, another assembles the blocks and heads, and another makes the final assembly. The factory produces over 100,000 engines a year, yet it has a relatively simple organization. The factory deals with few external variables. Its contacts are limited to the steel and machine shop industry. Contrast the Saab engine factory with a rather small voluntary enterprise such as Federation of Churches in a metropolitan area with only 20 employees. Yet it operates over 50 different projects, utilizing 2,000 volunteers, touching such aspects of community life as education, health, family life, communications, public welfare, and politics. It involves all aspects of the city from the illiterate poor to the country club power brokers. Its combinations and permutations are much larger, and its environment much more volatile and unpredictable than that faced by the Saab factory.

As each new variable is added to the mix, the possible solution to a given problem can expand exponentially. When you add the difficulty of measuring so many factors to the unknown elements and to all the variables, such a line of possibilities emerges that the problem defies solution. Tracy Connors comments: "This cannot be overemphasized. This fact is often unrecognized or appreciated by board members who, more often than not, come from profit-making backgrounds."[112]

The tendency of voluntary enterprises to accumulate multiple purposes immediately presents management with a complex situation. The enterprise must go in more than one direction simultaneously. Though it is strongly motivated and purposeful by nature, the goals are complex and not always unified. The Boston Consulting Group wrote:

> The problem of identifying optimal policies and potential strategies in a voluntary enterprise must be inherently more complex. In fact, most institutions would find their planning and policy formulation much easier if they were profit-making organizations. Then at least they would have a common denominator for their objectives and strategies.[113]

The role of voluntarism immediately gives the leadership at least two distinct groups with which to deal to accomplish objectives. At least two sets of motivators, two methods of directing, and two systems for controlling the work are required. Paid employees and unpaid volunteers are unequally yoked, and managing the two groups in tandem adds greatly to organizational complexity. You might be able to harness an ox or a stallion individually to pull a wagon, but with voluntary enterprises, the two must work together.

The presence of a constituency and the need to function politically increases complexity. There are many factions to satisfy. Efforts toward developing cohesion and support can pull counter to efforts toward goal achievement. The enterprises not only have a number of vertical hierarchical levels but also many subsystems with intertwining relationships on each level. Robert M. Schaffner, writing in *Management Review*,[114] described his reactions as a scientific/technical executive in a new career. Outside the profit-seeking sector, he discovered more complexity, largely due to the many new horizontal relationships in his new organizational environment.

The lack of the integrating contribution of money and of profit-and-loss measurements to monitor operational effectiveness makes management even more complex. The interaction between resource allocation and performance is less direct.

The existence of voluntary enterprise's two internal systems—one for providing services and the other for developing resources—automatically multiplies the complexity. It affects the organizational structure, internal relationships, and incentives, and works against efforts to simplify management. The personnel and management style necessary to deal with "other-directed" individuals adds more variables to the pot, as does the wide range of available resources.

In addition, consider the open systems, the abstract nature of the goals, the high tendency toward entropy, the relative autonomy of components, and the tendency to be transcendental, and you see the great complexity.

The impact of this characteristic on management is as profound as any other. Good management is usually sees as the antithesis of complexity. The competent manager searches constantly for explanations that simplify. He looks for patterns to find simpler structures. He looks for that which has already been encountered, analyzed, or solved elsewhere. He moves from qualitative observations to explanations that account for observed relationships. He seeks generality and predictability, relating his observations to similar events. He constantly seeks simplification so that he can anticipate problems, take action, and accurately predict results.

In planning, the manager seeks to reduce uncertainty. In organizing, he works toward increasing the orderly meshing of components and toward increasing competence and harmony while reducing chaos and conflict. In directing, the manager works toward increasing the application of energy to objectives, while reducing the dissipation of energy. And in controlling, he seeks to increase responsiveness and reduce confusion.

Complexity complicates all these efforts and makes good management more difficult to attain. Complexity adds variables, increases choices, makes outcomes less predictable, requires a wide range of skills, builds a labyrinth around leaders, and tends to confuse their concentration on objectives by putting an array of controls in their hands. It is difficult to drive a charging team of horses while juggling handfuls of reins. The great complexity in organizations of the voluntary sector loads a heavy burden on the manager's skill.

Aspects of Complexity

There is one positive aspect of the complexity in voluntary enterprise management: It's never dull.

Complexity creates a special kind of organizational environment that is great for those who thrive in such a climate. The many options, the unpredictable outcomes, the multivariables, and the compounded human relationships appeal to some people. They thrive on challenge. They are nourished by a constant diet of intermingled tasks and intertwined expectations. Laocoön hardly seems to be enjoying his plight. But everyone is not a Laocoön. Among our population you will occasionally find a guy like Mike.

I met Mike in 1967 when I stopped in Letecia, Colombia, on a trip deep into the trackless Upper Amazon jungle. He runs a variety of businesses in this remote outpost of civilization. Among them is the capturing of Amazon animals for zoos. Mike likes to wrestle anacondas, the largest of tropical snakes. Since then, I have often seen him pictured in magazines or on television, wallowing in mud and water in a Laocoön-like struggle with the serpent. Unlike Laocoön, Mike always wins, and he enjoys the struggle. In my consulting with organizations, I meet a lot of people like Mike, who enjoy their struggles with complex organizations.

On the negative side, however, voluntary enterprise managers have their hands full. A manager requires special and wide-range skills to deal successfully with the problems of complexity. He must be able to grasp and control many reins simultaneously. Like Ben Hur, galloping around the Hippodrome, fighting off his competitors, simultaneously reining in and urging on his four matched stallions, the manager must maintain the torturous pace until he surges across the finish line. The manager will deal with several management lines and systems, handle a variety of relationships and roles, and orchestrate various functions and tasks. He must be strong in political and diplomatic skills, and be sensitive to social as well as financial and programmatic criteria. The personality and image of the manager is often the linchpin, holding diverse segments and factors together. So complexity places a heavy load on the manager's shoulders and exerts much pressure on his psyche and his capability.

Complexity also strains the capacity of the organization's various problem-solving mechanisms. A computer specialist, working on a regional not-for-profit organization with me, commented, "The problems are simply not programmable, and if they were, they are so nonrepetitive that you might solve all of them today, and with the passage of a little time they would have an entirely new set of unique ones." Decisions are difficult to deal with in terms of numerical variables and algorithms conducive to decision making on a numerical basis. There is not a lot of control over organizational components, and the ratio of "data required for decisions" to "data obtainable" is great. You have a mixed bag of goals, expectations, and preferences, and must constantly work toward consensus. Since problem solving operates at all levels, the complexity makes this a pervasive problem.

Another aspect has to do with personnel. One business is somewhat like another in that management's relationship to its human resources is the same—to paid employees. Paid voluntary enterprise managers deal with their employees, but also with policy- and management-level volunteers, direct-service volunteers, and resource-development volunteers. Contributors might be still another set of individuals. Each group has its own needs and its own motivations. Accountability is different, and often interrelated, for each group. Cecily Selby, writing in the *Harvard Business Review,* notes that individuals in parallel paid and volunteer positions are often frustrated and feel impotent, "with a concomitant decline in effort and creativity."[115] She says that both accountability and satisfaction are diffused. "The confused management line is one reason why many organizations . . . spend so much time on analysis of structure rather than on service." She says that the "consideration of bylaws, reorganization, and planning for planning—rather than analysis of program, of service, indeed, of what the organization is in business for—consumes meeting after meeting." Selby says that this can lead to two extremes of control: "domination by a determined executive, or a state of participatory democracy that renders responsiveness to need and adaptation to change so slow as to be ineffective."

The markets also contribute to complexity. There is a market for the organization's services: its clients and potential clients. Then, there are the contributors and potential contributors, and the volunteer workers and potential volunteers. One internal system markets services to one group, while the second system seeks to appeal to its market: the sources of resources.

Management amid Complexity

The voluntary enterprise manager may be likened to a juggler. But instead of juggling a number of identical balls, he must juggle dissimilar objects—some light, some heavy; some small, some large; some round, some odd-shaped. Perhaps more accurately, he can be compared to the ramrod in a western trail drive. Only instead of cattle, his herd is a motley mixture of cattle, sheep, elephants, dogs, and fowl. Some of his drovers are hired hands, while others drift into and out of their duties as their time allows. Others want only to herd the sheep, others the cattle, and only rarely do they all agree on the same trail to take. The complexity of voluntary enterprises makes heavy demands upon their managers. All else being equal, the demands are in the form of a broad range of skills and the ability to deal with complexity.

"Burnout" can be a problem. While complexity provides enough variety to hold boredom at bay, it exacts a heavy toll in energy and stress. Tracy Connors[116] reports that a survey on the needs of one group of not-for-profit managers showed that the first-place problem was executive burnout. He feels, "We are burning out or running off some of our very talented people because we are asking too much of them." Financial rewards are rarely in proportion to the magnitude of success, and retirement provisions (if they exist at all) are far from plush. The executive under the stress of complexity will seek relief in outside conferences and seminars that take him away from daily routine. Out-of-town trips give him both a sense of perspective and a breather from regular duties. He may throttle back on the amount of energy he puts into his work in order to reduce his level of stress and make the load tolerable. The demands of the constituency are such that it could be more difficult for him than for his business counterpart to disassociate himself from the operations of the organization.

Confronted with a built-in tendency toward complexity, management must simplify whatever can be simplified, and develop sound approaches for dealing with what must remain complex. In reviewing your management process, it is wise to sort out those aspects subject to simplification and those that are irreducible. Every change should be in the direction of reducing variables. No one needs to foster complexity; the normal order of things will generate complexity aplenty. As many changes as are effective should be made from the complex to the simple, from the abstract to the concrete, from the broad to the narrow. Such efforts will help counter the tendency to expand from the simple toward greater complexity.

But the manager walks in fine line. Complexity will remain a reality, and a search for simplicity can be overdone. Efforts to simplify by narrowing problems down into more easily understood models could cloud reality. You are often in a dilemma: Do you try to cope with overwhelming complexity, or with the unworkable nature of oversimplified solutions based on unrealistic models? Such social systems are difficult to model. Their variables are almost impossible to define. In building the organization toward simplicity, you must be content with reducing its complexity. It can never be eliminated.

What cannot be simplified must be dealt with. It is inevitable that the organizational leadership will grow in its skills in managing complexity. A first step, perhaps, is an acknowledgment of the variables and the fact that a change in one part of the system affects the entire system. The more you understand the influence of the variables in the system and their effect upon the whole, the better you can forecast. A complex open system will never be as predictable as a more simple closed one, but each step toward reducing uncertainty is a progressive step.

Complexity affects decision making in all the major management functions. As discussed previously, the many variables make it difficult to define measurable objectives and forecast results. Organizing is difficult because of the many horizontal relationships, and the interrelationships of paid and volunteer personnel. Often it is difficult to prepare an organization chart on one sheet of paper. (An overlay showing how one structure related to another might be advisable. In effect, you have a three-dimensional rather than a two-dimensional structure.) Coordination is an especially important function in complex organizations. It serves as a linchpin between one task groups and another. One of the most difficult problems in controlling the work is in resolving conflicts among alternatives and calculating their relative worth when the alternatives have multidimensional attributes.

Internal communications are especially critical in a complex organization. While good communications will not substitute for good organization, they can go a long way in compensating for gaps, assisting in coordination, and strengthening cohesion among units. A careful analysis will identify the various publics that need to communicate with each other. An intentional effort should be made to select an efficient medium for each communication task. Communications should not be left to chance. Whether the medium be a newsletter for the constituents or a weekly meeting of department heads, it should provide for an optimum two-way flow. Communication means listening to feedback just as much as statements and directives.

Formal communications channels are not the only means of transferring information. The informal networks also play an important role. A wise manager will not waste his energy on efforts to squelch the informal "grapevine" networks. It is an impossible task. Energies will be better spent in feeding communication's hungers with accurate and interesting information through both formal and informal channels.

Communication in many voluntary enterprises includes more than factual data. It also serves the purpose of inspiring, motivating, and building cohesion. Personnel constantly need to be reminded of the organization's traditions, purposes, and objectives. Praise for the good work of both individuals and task groups is part of the reward system of the enterprise. Media that are organizationwide stimulate interpersonal communications and play a direct part in bonding individuals to their groups and groups to the total enterprise. The communications networks are the nerve system of the organization. When they work well in a complex entity, the many parts are linked into a manageable whole.

Complex voluntary enterprises can be made more manageable by reducing the complexity of that which can be simplified, and by developing skills for dealing with the remaining inevitable complexity.

Conclusion

A novice, upon his first glance at a game of checkers and a game of chess, will be struck by the games' apparent similarity. Each is played with 16 white and 16 black "men," and the boards are identical and interchangeable. But the two games have different objectives and are played in different ways, and chess is more complex than checkers.

Persons accustomed to business and industry are often dismayed by what they perceive as confusion when they observe the operations of voluntary enterprises. The business people are like checker players looking at a chess game, who are dismayed to see a piece moved backward or another moved two squares to the left and one square forward; they become disoriented when they see pieces "jumped" without being captured. What they see in the not-for-profit environment is not incompetence or mismanagement but a different kind of game—a game in which complexity and ambiguity are endemic.

The multiple purposes of voluntary enterprises, their dual internal systems, their achievement of objectives by both volunteer and paid personnel, the lack of measurability, and other variables help create this complexity.

Complexity may indeed reduce boredom, but it certainly increases frustration. The more complex the organization, the greater the challenge its leaders face to achieve smooth systematic management. Except for providing an environment for executives who enjoy uncertainty, complexity has little that is good to offer to leadership. It overloads managers, strains the capacity of the organization's problem-solving mechanism, complicates the motivation and supervision of personnel, and creates marketing difficulties. The manager must become a master juggler with many dissimilar objects in the air at once.

How do you cope with such an environment? How do you avoid burnout, maintain your inner equilibrium, and simultaneously progress toward solving daily the ever-changing Rubik's Cube of a voluntary enterprise?

One helpful procedure is to simplify everything that can be simplified. Every change should be toward reducing variables, moving from the abstract to the concrete, and pinning down as many loose ends as possible. By intentionally simplifying what can be simplified, more energy is released and made available to apply to the complexity that will remain.

Organizational leadership must acknowledge the inevitability of complexity. There is no technique or procedure that will eradicate it. It comes with the territory. Accepting complexity as inevitable, the leadership should develop policies, procedures, and skills for dealing with it. While an open complex system can never be as prodictable and manageable as a closed system, it provides a wide range of relationships and has the capacity for achieving objectives and dealing with them in depth.

Coordination is a vital concurrent management function dealing with complexity. Coordination links the various parts to ensure that interference among the various organizational elements is minimized and that synergism is maximized. Internal communications also assume a vital role. Good internal communication is essential in the complex organizational environment. Both the formal structures and the informal communication networks should be fully utilized in tying together the disparate elements of the enterprise, guiding the various task groups, and motivating the entire mass to move forward together.

As in chess, the choices are rarely obvious. There are many options available. Each piece has a different value, moves in a different way, and poses a different threat. The game cannot be mastered in a short timespan, neither does it ever cease to present a new situation and instruct the player in appropriate responses.

17

WHERE DO YOU GO FROM HERE?

Voluntary enterprises flourish where government is unwelcome and where business cannot survive. The voluntary not-for-profit sector is indispensable to our way of life. If it were banished today, we would recreate it tomorrow. The voluntary spirit flavors our society, nourishes the sector's constituents, and spices the lives of millions of individuals. Yet its present posture is nothing compared with the power to enrich that lies latent within its corpus. Like Gulliver bound to the ground by the threads of the Lilliputians, it lives, breathes, and stirs within its bonds. In my opinion, it yearns for the unleashing that only the right quality of management will provide.

A Sector of Opportunity

The voluntary sector's centerpiece is its capacity for expressive as well as instrumental ends. Voluntary enterprises possess the ability to maintain an environment in which their members can legitimately foster their own interests and satisfy needs that made membership in them desirable in the first place.

The wonderful organizations in this sector do not have to be predictable or profitable or even practical. They are free to explore on the cutting edge, and have both the flexibility to innovate and the endurance to persevere down the tunnel, even when no light is evident at the other end. They constantly enrich the soil of our society so that organizations from all three sectors may prosper. They can function and even prosper in an ambience of ambiguity and uncertainty. Within their rich mixture of forces and personalities and ideas and needs, concepts collide and spawn marvelous innovations. Since they do not have to produce a profit, they are the ideal vehicles for individuals to band together to accomplish a wide variety of purposes. They are the means by which diverse motivations find expression to reach significant ends that enrich life.

Voluntary enterprises have access to vast amounts of human energy through quality time and voluntarily contributed effort, funds and talent. They are a means of amplifying the voices of their constituents for myriad causes, and they provide avenues of expression available nowhere else. Though they often bewail their lack of funds, their very freedom from the absolute necessity of cost-effectiveness authorizes them to explore uncharted territory.

Within the voluntary enterprise environment, pure democracy can flourish. What a marvelous training ground exists in their committees, intrigues, human interplay, personal influence, and meetings, meetings, meetings. Nowhere else will you find human values so emphasized. Human beings are what such organizations are all about; we are something more than organizational machinery and the amassing of material goods.

Those who work full time in the voluntary sector have boundless resources for personal satisfaction and the practice of our professions. The bonds are not so tight that we are seriously frustrated or inhibited. The voluntary enterprise is adaptable, responsive to creativity and new approaches and specialized interests. Sanction is given to "glory in the doing." Most of these organizations have an invigorating vitality, with a great amount of simultaneous activity. They are one of the primary creators of civilization and one of civilization's greatest creations.

But as with any effort that accomplishes anything significant, there must be discipline. Individuals must discipline themselves with self-control, and the organizations must discipline themselves with effective and appropriate management. If their causes are to prevail, their services are to accomplish their purposes, and their participants are to find enduring satisfaction, the enterprises must seize opportunities and solve problems.

Important Sequential Management Functions

Some solutions address more than a single problem. As I have identified unique management problems and opportunities in the voluntary sector, I have called your attention to implications and posed a variety of steps you might take. Often the solution to one problem is also the solution to another. In this concluding chapter, I will swing my spotlight away from causes and focus it upon key general management procedures that are essential to effective not-for-profit enterprises.

Examine your present process for eliciting and channeling your organizational energy, modify it to include my suggestions, and you will have opened the door to a more effectively managed organization. The first procedures I will summarize are sequential functions, activities that are built into the management systems in sequence.

One advantage that business organizations enjoy is their more precise measure of output. They can use their profit-and-loss measures to evaluate the contribution made by virtually every unit in the company. Their purpose is clear and unambiguous. Though the not-for-profit manager will not likely duplicate these advantages, he may move his organization's management process toward more precise measurable objectives and thus reduce uncertainty. As valid and meaningful units of service are identified and utilized in the planning, organizing, staffing, coordinating, guiding, and controlling of organizational tasks, the fog will dissipate. Many disagreeable birds can be killed with the one stone. The quantifiable unit of service integrated into objectives and purpose is often an adequate stand-in for the profit measure of business.

But beware. Keep the voluntary enterprise a voluntary enterprise. Try to run a nonbusiness exactly like a business and you will end up with something like Grape Nuts—neither grapes nor nuts. At best you will sire a second-rate business. The voluntary sector is worth your commitment. You need only improve the way it is managed. Develop quantifiable units and objectives that are truly congruent with the organizational purpose. Use them as management tools. But retain the character of the voluntary sector. If your purposes defy measurement, do not throw away your purpose for the lack of a tool. The best things are often unmeasurable.

Another conclusion that reared its head in many of the earlier chapters was the need to intentionally and systematically evaluate the organization's posture against its purpose. Not-for-profit enterprises drift off course easily. They tend to accumulate multiple purposes. The tail regularly tries to wag the dog. Often the officially stated purpose of the organization is not the true *ad hoc* purpose. Often its very valid expressive purposes are unwritten and even unspoken. This allows for much hypocrisy and game-playing in which the organization's pronouncements and practice do not mesh. To know where it is going, the organization needs to agree on a written purpose as well as on written objectives and strategies to move everyone forward together toward that purpose.

But these written statements are not to be enshrined in isolation. They are tools, like a ship's compass, to be watched by the helmsman and periodically checked by the captain. If the owners, passengers, captain, and crew want to change course, they may do so. But until they do, they must periodically measure their direction against their destination.

It is all right for a ship to have more than one destination, and for voluntary enterprises to have more than one purpose. One passenger may undertake a voyage both to go to Rio and to get a suntan by the ship's pool. Another may wish to go to Rio and read *War and Peace* on the way. Another may want to get off at Port of Spain. But there must be priorities. In the case of the entire organization, these priorities should be ordered and ranked into a hierarchy of purposes. Number three is abandoned if number two is in trouble. Number two is not addressed until progress toward number one is on target.

The two systems, one for developing resources and the other for providing services, profoundly affect not-for-profit management. Neither can be neglected. The two must be coordinated. They may require two organizations and two marketing plans. For true progress, do not depend on the incidental interest generated by the service-providing system to limit the development of resources. Set coordinated goals for each system and intentionally allocate an appropriate amount of "seed money" so that each may reach its objectives.

The needs and demands of the constituency give the organizations their politically charged social character. This distinctive character should be accepted as the nature of the creature. It is in the genes. Selection of staff, design of the organization chart, method of decision making, guidance of workers, and control of the work must be appropriate for this kind of organization. Monitor the relationships between paid staff and volunteers at all levels. Include the volunteers and constituency in the communications system and in the sequence of the management process; recognize that implementation may take more time than in a utilitarian or coercive organization.

Because of the constituency, the law, and the position our voluntary enterprises enjoy in our society, vast resources exist for them to do their job. Do not rely on chance in order to tap them. Develop a system for identifying your needs and potential sources.

Important Concurrent Management Functions

In addition to the sequential management functions that are built into any management process at specific points, you also exercise a variety of concurrent functions. They consist of activities that take place all of the time, at all levels, and by all the leaders. Among these, of special importance to the voluntary enterprise, are the following;

Inspiration/Persuasion.   Apply the motivation power of the organizational purpose to all task levels. Build resolve and confidence. Organizational participants do not work because they have to or for material rewards; you must feed the hungers that motivate them.

Bonding.   Build cohesion to integrate newcomers into task groups and into the organization as a whole and to confirm and further commit existing members.

Focusing Attention on Results.   The nature of a profit-seeking business provides this focus almost automatically. A not-for-profit organization can easily focus all its energy on its process and inputs. Therefore, the leadership must persistently draw attention to the high-priority result desired.

Encouraging Creativity.   Potential human and material resources are so great, and economical and novel avenues for service so abundant, that innovations are often applicable at all levels. Everyone associated with the organization should be busy identifying resources and foraging for fresh ideas.

Managers in all kinds of not-for-profit enterprises are beginning to appreciate the importance of their commonality. They are a special breed who bring broad talents to their tasks. Those of us who have the rewarding and challenging job of managing these organizations should accelerate the movement toward recognizing our management as a distinctive specialty. We can all gain. We can all contribute. We can make all of our organizations more effective and productive.

REFERENCES

1. Alexis de Tocqueville, *Democracy in America* (New York: Vantage Books, 1955), as quoted in Bernard M. Kapell, "The Volunteer Movement in the United States," *Volunteer Administration* 2 (3) (1969), p. 11.
2. Joseph J. Thorndike, Jr., and Joseph Kastner, eds., *Life's Picture History of Western Man* (New York: Time, Inc., 1941), p. 286.
3. Ibid, p. 286.
4. Ibid, p. 286.
5. Frederick Jackson Turner, *The Frontier in American History* (New York: Henry Hult, 1937), as quoted in Thorndike and Kastner, p. 287.
6. President Ronald Reagan, Address to the National Alliance of Business, Sheraton Washington Hotel, Washington, D. C., 5 October 1981.
7. "31% in Poll Say They Engage in Volunteerism," *The New York Times,* Sunday, 18 October 1981, p. 37.
8. Kenn Allen, "Volunteering in America," *Voluntary Action Leadership* (Winter, 1982), pp. 18–20.
9. Robert Gatewood and James Lahiff, "Differences in Importance of Job Factors between Managers in Voluntary and Profit Organizations," *Journal of Voluntary Action Research* 6 (3–4) (1977), p. 133.
10. Amitai Etzioni, *A Comparative Analysis of Complex Organizations* (New York: Free Press, 1975), pp. 40–41.
11. David S. Adams, "Voluntary Action: Speculations on the Thing Itself," *Volunteer Administration* 9 (1) (1976), pp. 8–12.
12. Quoted by Reagan, 1981.
13. Edmund G. Brown, Jr., "The Importance of a Voluntary Society," *Voluntary Action Leadership* (Winter, 1978), p. 46.
14. Ralph M. Kramer, *Voluntary Agencies in the Welfare State* (Berkeley: University of California Press, 1981), p. 212.
15. Humble, "Management of the Non-Profit Organization," in *Drucker/Humble Workshop* (Rockville, Maryland: BNA Films, 1977).
16. Etzioni, p. 29.
17. Suzanne Garment, "Who Will Answer Reagan's Call for Volunteers?" *The Wall Street Journal,* 2 October 1982, p. 24.

18. Peter F. Drucker, *Management: Tasks, Responsibilities, Practices* (New York: Harper & Row, 1974), p. 9.
19. Malcolm Walker, Taped interview, San Antonio, Texas, 1979.
20. "The Non-Profit Motive," *Forbes*, 13 November 1978.
21. Ibid.
22. Richard Cornuelle, *Reclaiming the American Dream* (New York: Random House, 1965), p. 49.
23. David E. Mason, "The Distinctive Nature of Voluntary Organization Management," *Voluntary Action Leadership* (Spring 1979), pp. 2–3.
24. Horace, *Satires*.
25. Walker, 1979.
26. Secretary Moon Landrieu, Taped interview, Washington, D.C., 1979.
27. John P. Van Gigch, *Applied General Systems Theory* (New York: Harper & Row, 1974), pp. 126–127.
28. Kramer, p. 169.
29. James Naughton, Videotaped interview, Washington, D.C., 1982.
30. Herbert Heaton, *Productivity in Service Organizations* (New York: McGraw-Hill, 1977), p. 175.
31. William Shakespeare, *Macbeth*, Act II, sc. 1, line 16.
32. Ella Wheeler Wilcox, "The Winds of Fate," in *The Best Loved Poems of the American People*, ed. Hazel Felleman (Garden City, NY: Doubleday, 1936).
33. "Ph.D. Phoolery" (editorial), *The Wall Street Journal*, 18 August 1981.
34. Herbert Spencer, *Social Statistics* (New York: D. Appleton & Co., 1896).
35. Kenneth Boulding, "General Systems Theory: The Skeletons of Science," (April 1956), pp. 197–208.
36. As quoted in John Fisher, *How to Manage a Non-Profit Organization* (Toronto: Management and Fund-Raising Centre, 1978), p. 1.
37. David Horton Smith, "The Impact of the Non-Profit Voluntary Sector of Society," in *The Non-Profit Organization Handbook*, ed. Tracy D. Connors (New York: McGraw-Hill, 1980), pp. 1-22.
38. Peter Drucker, p. 246.
39. Abraham H. Maslow, *Motivation and Personality* (New York: Harper, 1954).
40. Lindy Boggs, Taped interview, New Orleans, 1979.
41. Jon Van Til, Taped interview, New Orleans, 1981.
42. Heaton, p. 116.
43. Etzioni, p. 115.
44. Adam Smith, *The Wealth of Nations* (New York: Dutton, 1960), as quoted in Fisher, p. 67.
45. David Horton Smith, pp. 1–3.
46. David S. Adams, "Volunteer Action: Speculations on the Thing Itself," *Journal of Volunteer Administration* 9 (1) (1976), pp. 8–12. Copyright 1976 by the Association for Volunteer Administration. Reprinted by permission.
47. Richard Cornuelle and Robert Finch, *The New Conservative Liberal Manifesto* (San Diego: Viewpoint Books, 1968), p. 115.
48. Max Wortman, "A Radical Shift from Bureaucracy to Strategic Management in Voluntary Organizations" (Unpublished paper, Virginia Polytechnic Institute, 1980).
49. Dan Fenn, "Executives as Community Volunteers," *Harvard Business Review* (March–April 1971), p. 156.

50. Benjamin DeMott, "The Day the Volunteer Didn't," *Psychology Today*, March 1978, p. 23.
51. *The New York Times*, 1981.
52. Wortman, 1980.
53. Etzioni, p. 40.
54. Kramer, p. 206.
55. Ibid.
56. Tracy D. Connors, ed., *The Non-Profit Organization Handbook* (New York: McGraw-Hill, 1980), section 3, part 1, chap. 1.
57. "Boys' Town Bonanza," *Time*, 10 April 1972, pp. 17–18.
58. Cornuelle, 1965, p. 52.
59. Ibid, p. 52.
60. Drucker, p. 146.
61. Lindy Boggs, 1979.
62. Murray Fincher, Taped interview, Madisonville, Louisiana, 1979.
63. George Odiorne, *Management by Objectives* (Belmont, California: George S. Pitman, 1975), p. 164.
64. Cornuelle, pp. 211–212.
65. David Horton Smith, pp. 1-31–1-32.
66. Dean Kelley, Taped interview, Cleveland, Ohio, 1981.
67. "Big Profits in 'Non-Profits,'" *Reader's Digest*, April 1979, pp. 169–174.
68. Kelley, 1981.
69. "How to Apply for Recognition of Exemption for an Organization," IRS Publication No. 557.
70. Kelley, 1981.
71. Harvey Katz, *Give! Who Gets Your Charity Dollar?* (Garden City, New York: Anchor Press/Doubleday, 1974).
72. Etzioni, p. 192.
73. Paul White, Sol Levine, and George Vlasak: "Exchange as a Conceptual Framework for Understanding Interorganizational Relationships: Applications to Non-Profit Organization," in *Organization Theory in an Interorganizational Perspective* (Kent, Ohio: Kent State University, The Comparative Administration Research Institute of the Center for Business and Economic Research, 1971), p. 44.
74. William Ouchi, *Theory Z, How American Business Can Meet the Japanese Challenge* (Reading, Mass.: Addison-Wesley, 1981).
75. Dale McConkey, *MBO for Non-Profit Organizations* (New York: AMACOM, 1975), p. 39.
76. "Rocky, the End of a Dynasty," *Look*, 19 February 1979, p. 57.
77. Senator George McGovern, Televised interview, New Orleans, 1981.
78. Landrieu, 1979.
79. Ibid.
80. McGovern, 1981.
81. Landrieu, 1979.
82. McGovern, 1981.
83. Wall Frazier, *Andrew Carnegie* (London: Oxford University Press, 1970), p. 658.
84. Hal Rainey, "Comparing Public and Private Organizations," *Public Administration Review* (March–April 1976).
85. Jan Hall, "What Makes a Good Manager Good, Bad, or Average?" *Psychology Today*, August 1976, pp. 52–55.

86. Howard Foshee, Taped interview, Nashville, Tennessee, 1979.
87. John R. P. French and Bertram Raven, "The Basis of Social Power," in *Group Dynamics*, 2nd ed., ed. Dorwin Cartwright and A. F. Zander (Evanston, Illinois: Row, Peterson, 1960), pp. 607–623.
88. Abraham Zaleznik, "Power and Politics in Organizational Life," *Harvard Business Review* (May–June, 1970), pp. 47–60.
89. Susan Ellis, Taped interview, San Antonio, Texas, 1979.
90. Howard Foshee, 1979.
91. Max Wortman, Taped interview, New Orleans, 1981.
92. Michael Maccoby, *The Leader* (New York: Simon & Schuster, 1981), p. 1.
93. Etzioni, p. 435.
94. James R. Rawls, Robert A. Ullrich, and Oscar Nelson, Jr., "A Comparison of Managers Entering and Reentering the Profit and Nonprofit Sectors," *Academy of Management Journal* 18 (3) (1973), pp. 616–623.
95. Herbert Hicks and Ray Gullett, *Organizations: Theory and Behavior* (New York: McGraw-Hill, 1975), p. 380.
96. Malcolm Knowles, *The Adult Learner: A Neglected Species* (Houston, Texas: Gulf Publishing Co., 1973), p. 17.
97. Max Wortman, "A Radical Shift."
98. Etzioni, p. 358. A. W. Gouldner, "Cosmopolitans and Locals: Toward an Analysis of Latent Social Roles," *Administrative Science Quarterly* 2 (1957), pp. 281–306. H. L. Wilensky, *Intellectuals in Labor Unions* (Glencoe, Ill.: Free Press, 1956).
99. Cecily Selby, "Better Performance from Non-Profits," *Harvard Business Review* (September–October, 1978), p. 93.
100. Michael Maccoby, *The Gamesman, the New Corporate Leaders* (New York: Simon & Schuster, 1976).
101. Rawls, Ullrich, and Nelson, 1973, p. 620.
102. Robert Gatewood & James Lahiff, p. 196.
103. Ibid.
104. Robert R. Blake and Jane S. Mouton, *The New Management Grid* (Houston: Gulf Publishing, 1968).
105. Drucker, *Management* p. 411.
106. Etzioni, p. 355.
107. Tracy Connors, Taped interview, New Orleans, 1981.
108. Alan Andreasen, Taped interview, New Orleans, 1981.
109. Peter Spurney, Televised interview, New Orleans, 1981.
110. "Indian Education: A National Tragedy—A National Challenge," Report of the U.S. Senate Committee on Labor and Public Welfare, 1969, p. 19.
111. Virgil, *The Aeneid*, Bk. II, lines 217–224.
112. Connors, personal communication.
113. Robert Anthony and Regina Herzlinger, *Management Control in Non-Profit Organizations*, (Homewood, Illinois: Richard D. Irwin, 1975), p. 183.
114. Robert M. Schaffner, "Can a Scientific-Technical Executive from Industry Find Happiness in a Government Agency," *Management Review* (March 1975), p. 32.
115. Selby, 1978, p. 94.
116. Connors, Interview, 1981.

INDEX